Cover design by Lindsey Redstall from sketches made by
Mr. Chris Whitesides of a ghost seen by him in 1980 while coin
hunting at Trimley St. Mary. (See author's preface.)

GHOSTS OF
EAST ANGLIA

GHOSTS
OF
EAST ANGLIA

H. Mills West

COUNTRYSIDE BOOKS
NEWBURY, BERKSHIRE

First Published in 1984
by Barbara Hopkinson Books
© H. Mills West 1984
This edition published 1991

Reprinted 1999, 2002, 2003

COUNTRYSIDE BOOKS
3 CATHERINE ROAD
NEWBURY, BERKSHIRE

To view our complete range of books,
please visit us at
www.countrysidebooks.co.uk

ISBN 1 85306 067 4

Produced through MRM Associates Ltd., Reading
Printed in England by J. W. Arrowsmith Ltd., Bristol

Preface

It can happen to anyone. That is the most convincing lesson I have learned in seeking out these tales of East Anglian ghosts. Ghostly experiences do not belong to some separate, esoteric province half-obscured by superstition but happen to ordinary people following their everyday lives. Often it is a single experience in a lifetime but profound enough to be remembered in every detail. A fisherman returning to his home from Lowestoft; a young girl on a Saturday afternoon walk; a hairdresser at work in her salon; a bricklayer walking a field with a metal detector. Could circumstances be more mundane – and for this reason, more convincing?

In the case of the coin-hunter, Mr. Chris Whitesides, nothing could have been farther from his thoughts that autumn afternoon when, with permission from a local farmer, he walked the furrows of a ploughed field using his metal detector. There was a small wood ahead beyond a barbed wire fence and a man in an old-fashioned style of dress was standing there. Thinking it could be the farm manager, Mr. Whitesides decided to have a chat but when he was within a few yards of the figure, it vanished . . . impossible to scale the fence in a hurry or to disappear in any direction. Mr. Whitesides not only searched the area thoroughly but called out several times but there was no result. Very puzzled, he returned home and made a number of sketches of the figure he had so clearly seen, one of which has been reproduced for the cover picture.

I would like to thank Mr. Whitesides for his help and also those many people who have contributed from their own recollections, especially Miss Brooks, Mrs. Poulson, Mrs. Letch, Mrs. Cross, Miss Cooper, Mr. Weald, Mr. Warner, Mr. Lennard.

Besides these personal experiences, I have included some of the established ghost stories of the region and two or three long-ago legends, all of them chosen in consideration of a desire to present a series of entertaining stories. I hope you fill find them so.

H. Mills West.

Contents

Old Fleury

John Brooke, wickedest of country squires, built his house deep in the heathland of the Suffolk coast. The road that leads to it still wanders through gorse and bracken and apart from a macadamised surface gives few clues as to the modern age. Cars making for Walberswick, with its picturesque river and common, seldom go nearer than a mile or so of the place and those that venture along the narrow road for a picnic stop are not likely to go as far as the dead-end house of Blythburgh Lodge. I did, and hastily retreated from a barrage of shots from a dozen men standing with guns all around the Lodge. The fact that they were a party of farmers engaged in a pheasant shoot and not (I like to believe) aiming their twelve-bores at me, did not diminish my desire to get well away from a vicinity reputed to be deeply rooted in the violence of the past.

Along that road, long ago, galloped the wild young squire, an accomplished horseman and huntsman, landlord of many a scattered farm and cottage and the bane of all those unfortunate enough to be in lowly positions within his influence. Many there were who heard the approaching thunder of his galloping horse with fear and trepidation and cursed him inaudibly as he rode away. It was of little concern to the squire. He dealt with people in the same way that he treated his horse – with a wilful impatience by which neither animal nor human was spared.

1

The house, once called Westwood House, was finished in 1627 under John Brooke's own supervision, with stabling and coach housing added of a kind suitable for a man of his standing and rural pursuits. Thenceforward he came to spend little time in his house or in the company of his wife but was forever astride a horse and galloping furiously along the heath rides. The house and its many servants blessed his absences as fervently as those without wished him on his way.

On that fateful day that was the basis of the unnatural events to come, the squire followed the routine familiar to him, rising early, walking out with hunting crop in hand and dogs at heel to oversea some repairs being made to the Westwood House buildings. His manner was harsh, his decisions beyond question. Men worked for the squire through ignorance of any means of doing otherwise or knowledge of anything beyond the bounds of the rabbit-infested estate. As they trembled at his customary threats that morning, so did the poor litigants and minor wrong-doers at the court at Blythburgh tremble as they waited for his judgements due later in the day.

It was still early by some peoples' reckoning when the squire walked through the stables and, seeing nothing immediately worthy of castigation, ordered his favourite horse to be saddled for riding. Then, remembering that it was the day for the court and for travelling in more style he changed his mind and had the coach prepared. There was much in his thoughts about how he would deal with impudent poachers and such like who were unfortunate enough to come up before him.

While the coach and horses, all as shining and immaculate as two frightened young stablemen could make them, were being brought to the door, John Brooke went inside to prepare himself and don suitable accoutrements. It was at that time, in the midst of abusing such unfortunate servants as he came across, that he was attacked and delayed by a sudden unaccountable onset of pain. Despite its sharpness, he was constrained by his own nature not to give way to such weakness beyond a momentary pause and he called to his wife to help him put on his cloak.

However, the attack, of whatever kind it was, pressed heavily on him so that his wife and one or two friends who were staying in the house set themselves to dissuade him from making the journey that day. In and out of rages over pain and immobility he swore that he would go to Blythburgh or die. No matter that his condition became steadily worse, he railed and cursed at everything and everyone that would keep him here bound. In his last consciousness he heard the horses moving in the yard and whispered that he would ride again, whatever happened. The wicked squire died that same night in the same violent way that he had lived and no one could be certain of what cause.

An uneasy peace fell over the house after the funeral. Such oppression as John Brooke had shown, such close command of all the affairs of the estate and the neighbourhood, could not disappear over-night. An atmosphere remained in which servant girls shivered as they passed along the corridors of the upper floors of the house and in which they stayed over-long in the lighted kitchen after dark, unwilling to move. Already they had heard tales that Squire Brooke still rode that long and lonely road across the heath to Blythburgh as if from some supernatural compulsion to fulfill his last earthly intentions.

It was the parlour-maid who first saw the apparition within the house. Going to her room just before midnight along the corridor in which her master had had his bedroom, she saw the door thrown violently but noislessly open. What appeared then she tried to explain to her mistress, to whom she ran in a panic of fear. It was a rider, she said, a horseman but with no visible horse, an apparition that rode on a saddle swiftly along the corridor and out of sight but later returned and entered the room again.

Mistress Brooke comforted the hysterical girl as best she could and asked her if she would keep her description of the experience from the other servants lest they be frightened away. But the time soon came when there could be no more denying the visitations. They occurred frequently, always around midnight and always concerned the riding of an invisible horse back and forth along the corridors. The apparition seemed to originate, not simply in the master's bedroom but in a small inner room that he had used for some private purpose. When the haunting became so terrifying that no one would go near that part of the house, an unknowing builder was brought in to close the doorway of that hideous room with solid bricks.

Whether the ghostly rides continued after that date or whether the reputation and memory of those happenings were so strong that superstitious minds believed he still rode the corridor is difficult to determine but there was little comfort for those who lived there for generations after. Certainly the ghost became so familiar in the minds of local people that he was nicknamed Old Fleury.

Bricked up or not Old Fleury continued to rule. New servants as well as new occupants of the house together with the passing of time might well have prevailed against some lesser ghost but Old Fleury could not be flushed out nor disposed of as a feature of superstitious imagination. A determined effort to do so was made at one time when building alterations were being carried out and it was hoped to lay the old squire by the heels once and for all by opening up the inner room again and demonstrating its harmlessness.

With most of the household attending in various degrees of apprehension, the prosaic attack by hammer and chisel on the solid wall soon began. No one dared to look into that room of mystery until the screen was completely demolished. Then, in a moment, there were gasps and cries from the servants, some of whom hid in their rooms for the rest of the day. Even those considered to be modern and enlightened among the witnesses were horrified to discover that the room contained but two objects among the spiders webs and the dust. They were a saddle and a whip. And they were neither dusty nor touched by a single spiders web. In alarm the owners had the opening blocked up again at once but realised that they had lost to Old Fleury once again. Far from dispelling the servants' fears the episode ensured that from that day for a long time after they would refuse to walk along that ghostly corridor.

It seems that someone, however, had first removed the saddle and whip and it was resolved to burn them publicly in a great fire that would destroy their devilish qualities. Many people, who had long held some curiosity about Old Fleury came from the farms and cottages around and witnessed the saddle and the whip being thrown into the flames. And though there were some there who declared that they could see the squire still riding angrily in the firelight, from that time onwards there was to be no more than the memories and a certain atmosphere to plague the old house.

The Snettisham Mystery

What was the message, relayed from the spirit world, which was the subject of the mysterious confrontation in Snettisham church in 1893? The recipient of the instruction was a Mrs. Goodeve from London, who was bound to silence. All that the outside world knows, albeit in some detail, are the extraordinary events preceding that meeting. Its importance created an intensity of preparation in which ghostly presences in the likeness of their once living selves collaborated with earth-bound humans who, after all, have certain advantages over the immaterial world in the matter of communication, in working for the final exposition. In the end, despite the concluding mystery, all parties seem to have been satisfied, the feeling of intensity subsided and the spirits came no longer in the small hours to trouble the sleeping.

It all began, innocently enough, when Mrs. Goodeve decided to travel from her home in London to visit some friends in Bristol. This family happened to live in an old house locally reputed to be haunted though during the two years that they had lived there they had neither heard nor seen anything that would suggest the presence of spirits. It may be that they were people insensitive to such influences and to whom any kind of supernatural communication was difficult, for as soon as Mrs. Goodeve arrived a catalyst was provided by her psychical sympathies in which the

7

spirits became very active indeed.

On the very first night of her visit, Mrs. Goodeve woke suddenly, feeling that there was someone in the room. In the dim light she could make out the figure of a woman inside the door. Silently, the figure approached and leaned over the bed. Mrs. Goodeve could now see that the woman's head was covered with a shawl and that the face beneath the shawl was thin and infinitely sad, though with an underlying expression of kindness and understanding. Despite the circumstances, Mrs. Goodeve felt no fear at the sight of the apparition and when the woman said "Follow me" she was calm enough to light a candle and to follow the ghost into the dining-room next door. There the woman walked quickly across the room as if to keep beyond the candle-light and at the far end turned and looked at Mrs. Goodeve. The sad and emaciated face was illumined for a few moments. In a very deep voice, as if over-burdened with sorrow, the spectre said "To-morrow" and in an instant had disappeared.

Mrs. Goodeve returned to her bed and next morning she recounted her experience to the resident family. Her description of the ghostly visitor must have been very clear for the family recognised it at once as that of a Mrs. Seagrim, a former occupant of the house who had been in the habit of wearing an old Indian shawl over her head through a susceptibility to neuralgia. Feeling responsible for their guest's well-being the family tried to persuade her to change her bedroom. No one ever haunted them, they insisted, and they were quite willing to change places. But Mrs. Goodeve was not to be moved, feeling that somehow and by someone her help was desperately needed.

It was in the darkest hours of the next night that

Mrs. Goodeve woke to find the figure of the shawled woman at her bedside. "I have come as I promised," the spirit said in the same deep, sad voice. Mrs. Goodeve, still dazed from sleep but with no feeling of fright, sat up in bed and wanted to know: "Is this really happening or am I dreaming?"

The woman answered: "If you doubt that this is happening or if in the future you come to wonder if it was all some fancy of yours, I will tell you something that will prove that it is true. I was married on the 26th of September, 1860. When the time comes and if you still have doubts you can check this date in the church register. Now listen carefully."

As she listened, Mrs. Goodeve realised that there were other shadows moving in the darkness of the room. Behind the anxious, leaning figure of the woman now materialised the face and form of an old man, his whole appearance giving the impression of a long-standing and uncontrollable grief. As if reluctantly visible at first, this second ghost gradually developed from a mere prompter of the woman to be the dominant speaker and it was chiefly from this man that Mrs. Goodeve received the instructions that were ultimately to bring her to Snettisham and the completion of the quest.

First, however, there was much to understand and to remember. The old man seemed anxious to establish his living identity as a first step to gaining the credence of Mrs. Goodeve and gave his name as Henry Barnard. She could verify his existence, the ghost told her, by examining the church register at Snettisham in Norfolk and comparing the entries in his name with the dates and details which he now gave her. As with the woman, he seemed intensely concerned to involve

9

Mrs. Goodeve in a mission obviously important to their peace of mind.

As it happened, up to this moment in her life, Mrs. Goodeve had never heard of Snettisham and had no idea where it was. However, the ghosts insisted that she should pay a visit there, first to discover the registers and check the credentials of Mrs. Seagrim and Henry Barnard, then to follow the instructions which they gave her. Further tests of credibility were offered by the ghost of Henry Barnard in the form of predictions as to what would happen on the journey.

She must travel by rail, he told her, and she would find on her arrival at the destination that the appropriate out-going half of her ticket would not be taken by the ticket collector as would happen in the normal way. Moreover, she should not make any personal arrangements for accommodation since she would be offered assistance on her arrival by a dark man and she would lodge that night in the house of a woman whose child was buried in the same churchyard as Henry Barnard.

All this was told to Mrs. Goodeve on that second night of the haunting when the spectres gathered close beside her bed. It was not until later that she recalled that sometime during that visitation she was conscious that a third definable figure had joined the other two. It stood behind as if unwilling to be seen too closely but there came a few moments when she could see it quite clearly. It was the ghost of a man whose face was so deeply troubled that it struck her heart with pity, a face so full of grief that she could not bear to look at it. Throughout he only looked at her and did not speak nor was he identified by the others.

Mrs. Goodeve carefully remembered the detailed instructions for her journey. On the second day she must attend to the essential purpose of the visit. She must go to the church and explore the interior, committing to memory the features of aisles and columns. Following the South aisle to the South-west corner, she would find the tomb of Robert Cobb. That was the place of assignation. She must return there in the dark hours after midnight for, it was explained, the daylight drained the power of spirits and kept them hidden. When she returned to the church at midnight she would wait at the tomb of Robert Cobb and there she would be given the message that held the significance of all this preparation.

Accordingly, after this thorough briefing by the spirits, Mrs. Goodeve said goodbye to her Bristol friends and returned to her home in London. There she found out where Snettisham was situated, in a part of the country she had never visited before and a few days later she set out with some excitement and curiosity to discover what her strange excursion would yield. She had made no forward plans and arrived at the nearest station with no more preparation than a small, packed holdall. At once it seemed that she was under the control of the forces that the ghosts had foretold would usher her faithfully towards the accomplishment of the mission. All, in fact, turned out exactly as predicted. The station ticket-collector failed to detach the used half of her ticket and furthermore, hearing that she had no accommodation fixed, directed her to the house of the parish clerk, a man by the name of John Bishop.

It was John Bishop who came to the door when Mrs. Goodeve knocked, who welcomed her in and introduced her to his family. He was the dark man of the prophecies, she realised at once and gratefully ac-

11

cepted the hospitality offered. She must have disclosed her errand and described her experiences to John Bishop for on hearing her description of the second ghost he said at once: "That's Henry Barnard – he used to live hereabouts at a place called Cobb's Hall."

There was no need to enquire into the prediction that she would sleep in the house of a woman whose child was buried in the churchyard with Henry Barnard for on the following day during conversation with Mrs. Bishop she heard the full story of how their young daughter had drowned and had been buried there. So completely were the ghostly predictions fulfilled that it did not seem necessary at that time to verify the dates given. It was only at the very end of her visit that she decided to do so. All the dates and details were exactly as the ghosts had told.

Since the next day was Sunday, Mrs. Goodeve decided to make an initial acquaintance with the church by attending a service in company with John Bishop and his wife. Afterwards she walked about the edifice, inside and out, noting the tomb of John Cobb at the end of the aisle and preparing herself for the ordeal to come. Who would be waiting there in the dark at the dead of night? What did they expect of her and why had they chosen her as go-between? In her experience of psychic matters it had always been the living who sought communication with the dead but in this the spirits had initiated the transaction.

Because, for some reason they had been unable to reach a certain human, she must play the part of medium to translate the message the spirits wished to send. Was it something left unsaid, perhaps, before a life suddenly ended? Was it an urgent warning, a di-

12

rection for a hiding-place, a piece of information withheld too long? She could not guess. Whatever it was, it was something that lay heavily on the consciences of those no longer alive so that they were unable to rest.

That night, John Bishop brought her to the church again through the still and silent darkness of the hour between twelve and one o'clock. Their footsteps were loud and hurried on the gravel path and when they reached the great door it opened with a clang that went echoing among the grave stones. Mrs. Goodeve stood for a moment facing the gloom of the cavernous interior.

"You must not come in," she whispered. "Lock the door but stay nearby. When I am ready to come out I will give a knock."

She disappeared into the darkness and John closed and locked the door and waited in the chilly shadows of the porch. He could not imagine what was happening inside but once he started up thinking he heard voices. He would have unlocked the door then but the voices died away. A heavy silence followed so oppressive that the soft knock from inside surprised him when it came.

It could not have been more than about thirty minutes since she entered the church but now as Mrs. Goodeve emerged there was some new quality about her whole being. It did not require the daylight for John to recognise in her something newly calm and distant – as if she had been witness to something beyond normal understanding.

Yet, not then nor during the rest of her stay in Norfolk would she disclose anything of what had transpired at the tomb of John Cobb except that she had been given a vital message for the living daughter of

13

Henry Barnard. This she was required to deliver to her together with a rose from her father's grave, under vows of the utmost secrecy.

So far as public knowledge goes, the story ends there in Snettisham churchyard. There is no doubt that Mrs. Goodeve delivered the message without any loss of time to the proper person and privately for her ear alone. What it was we should not enquire too closely lest we disturb again those deeply worried ghosts who revealed themselves to Mrs. Goodeve in order to set that strange project in motion.

The Phantom Coach

Perhaps it is too much to say outright that Arthur Stokes and Jack Reeve were friends. They knew each other well and their paths often crossed in the rural environs of Southwold in those days when the horse had the undisputed right of the road. But, although they were both involved with horses, it was from quite opposite ends of the equine social scale and their casual meetings were usually occasions for some exaggerated badinage about each other's kind of horsemanship.

Most often the scoffing came from Jack Reeve who, after all, was the coachman at the Swan and had the experience of dealing with some of the finest horses in the county. The standard of turn-out of both horse and carriage from the Swan was the envy of all. By contrast, Arthur Stokes had no time to think of appearances. He drove the fish cart regularly from Southwold to Norwich and other likely markets at all times of the day and night and in all kinds of weather. Sometimes he would draw out of the way for a handsome coach to pass and find it was being driven by Jack Reeve who, as like as not, would hold his nose pointedly as the fish cart was passed.

Now and again Arthur would go down to the stables at the Swan and endure some good-natured raillery as the price of some advice or of a piece of harness that might be in danger of being thrown away. To be sure,

Jack enjoyed lording it on these occasions, putting a finishing polish to some piece of leather that already looked like burnished copper and making uncomplimentary remarks about the smell of fish. Arthur would take it all in good part. He knew his cart was as clean as water and elbow grease could make it and that his trips to Norwich were as speedy as any of his rivals.

It was during a visit to the Swan stables one autumn evening that Arthur remembered something that had puzzled him more than once on his journeys to Wangford and beyond. It was that piece of road alongside Reydon Hall, he told Jack, the piece they called Quay Lane. He had a master job getting his horse to go along that stretch of road at night and it seemed to be getting worse. He always avoided it when he could but occasionally time was important and he had to go that way. He wondered if Jack had found the same trouble along that stretch of road?

Jack was silent for a full minute, being of the kind to whom it is unnatural to admit to anything of which he is not firmly in control. Yes, he admitted casually, he'd heard something of the sort but he hardly ever went that way himself.

"I reckon it's the hedge," he said. "That blarm grut owd holly hedge all the way along one side o' the road. That's too high and that cast jolly grut shadders – enough to frighten any horse."

"Well there ain't much we can do about that," Arthur replied grimly. "Squire ain't likely to take that hedge down for the sake o' one or two jittery hosses. I shall atter go round the long way."

"Bad as that, is it?"

"Poor owd Boxer, he ain't easy to put out but I reckon he'd have bolted last time if I han't got down and led him along."

"Well, I'll try it myself one o' these nights," promised Jack loftily. "Just to see how one o' these carriage hosses take it."

The next day Arthur had to take a load of sprats to Norwich after dark. It was a drizzly night, cold and pitch black and it was difficult to see anything by the candle lanterns. Half the time he had to leave the driving to the horse's good sense and it seemed a dreary long journey before they reached Norwich. Even there the streets looked deserted and unwelcoming and Arthur was glad to get rid of his load and turn homeward again.

It was getting near midnight, he reckoned, before he had left Beccles well and truly behind him and it would be another hour or more yet before he could reach home and shelter from the rain. Sure enough, he could hear a church clock chiming one soon after they had clip-clopped through Wangford's empty village street. There would be no taking the long way round tonight in this weather but straight through Reydon and home. There would be a bowl of oats in his stall and a good straw bed for Boxer before his master could go to rest.

As they entered Quay Lane, black like a tunnel because of the high hedges, they had to drop down to walking pace. Even then, Boxer was uneasy, ears pricked high and nostrils quivering, walking unevenly and sometimes stopping altogether until nudged forward again. At a point in the road somewhere near the entrance to the Hall, the horse stopped again. Alternate threats and encouragement had no effect. The whip achieved nothing but a shivering of the horse's flanks.

17

Arthur felt the hair rising on the back of his neck as he heard somewhere ahead the wheels of a carriage with the accompanying sound of hurrying hooves. Suddenly Boxer shied, tried to pull sideways and jerked the wheels against the bank, all but throwing Arthur out of the cart. Then, as he regained his balance, he could see the cause of the fright.

Just ahead, at first shadowy in the gloom but soon well lighted from its own bright carriage lamps, was a coach of magnificent size with four horses now pulled up and standing silently. Arthur could easily make out the coachman sitting up on his box, a man dressed in the clothes of another age and yet somehow familiar as he sat there. But the close sight of the four horses, clear in the lamplight, took his mind from all other details. They were all black and they were all headless.

For a few moments the ghostly equipage was still, then the aged coachman seemed to become aware of the horse and cart ahead for he suddenly cracked his whip and the carriage turned aside and out of sight. Arthur could hear the whip and the sound of the wheels after they had disappeared but could not tell where they had gone for there was no room in the lane to pass.

What with shock and amazement, Arthur sat there for some time unable to move and it was Boxer who first showed a readiness to go ahead and make for home.

Next day in the Swan, Arthur told his story. The regulars sitting there showed no great surprise for the tale had been told before and in similar detail. The sound of wheels, a phantom coach and coachman materialising out of the darkness and the incredible horror of headless horses. It was something they did

18

not want to be reminded about and they sat and stared into their tankards in silence. Only one ancient villager took it on himself to add some observations on the mystery:

"O' course, you can't believe all the tales you hear, but when I was young they used to say someone was going to die when that old coach came along the lane. I do know there was an old rabbit catcher, Joe Gibbons – that was his name, he see the coach come along there one night and he took and had a heart attack and died. Right there in the lane. We know because his boy was with him and he see it too. I reckon it was on account o' this that the village women started the story that whenever the coach was seen someone was sure to die. O' course, we don't take too much notice of a tale like that nowadays – after all, someone is surely going to die sooner or later.

But I don't want to seem too clever. I had my fright at seeing that coach and horses nearly twenty years ago and I've never been along there in the dark since. But any rate, I'm still alive. That didn't kill me but I shouldn't want to see it again.

They used to say that was all on account o' some old squire who lived up at the Hall nigh on a hundred year ago. He was a cruel old devil – lord of the manor and lord over every poor creature living in the neighbourhood. When he was on his death-bed he begged to be forgiven for all his sins and prayed to be allowed to make some atonement. Those who were with him when he died told of how his prayers had been answered and that for penance he must drive his coach for all eternity. That don't seem a very likely story in these days but that's what they used to say and I suppose that's as good a reason as any."

A day or two later, Arthur came upon Jack at the smithy having one of the Swan horses shod and enjoying the leisure of watching the smith at work. To the accompaniment of ringing blows on metal and the familiar hiss and roar of the busy forge, Arthur told again his story of the frightening encounter he had had with the spectral coach. Jack's reaction was forthright and predictable.

"Bloody fancies," he swore. "Trees, shadows, a poor old hoss, a tired old man – that's all it adds up to. I tell you what – next time you take out your old fish cart I'll come along o' you with Daisy here and I'll go ahead o' you right along the lane."

"I don't know as I want to go along there again," Arthur objected mildly.

"What, are you going to have the jitters about that lane for the rest o' your life? You a mouse or something? When are you going to Norwich again?"

"Well, tomorrow night. Start about seven."

"Right. Tomorrow night at seven I'll personally escort you on your way till you get on to the main road. Don't you forget. I bet you'll find there's nothing in the lane but bats and bloody owls. And they won't stay long when they smell your old fish cart."

As usual, Jack's stronger personality carried the day. At the time and place appointed he duly turned up as promised and set off cheerfully on Daisy. It was a fine night but breezy and the branches overhead were moving enough to show a tattered moonlit sky. Arthur could just make out Jack riding ahead and even Boxer seemed to take courage from the pathfinder and followed without hesitation. Now and again Jack would be lost in the shadows ahead but then he would rein in and shout cheerfully through the darkness.

"Can't see no carriage. The only hoss I seen is old Daisy here and she's got her head on alright. We'll be on the main road soon and then I'll get back to the Swan."

Arthur breathed a sigh of relief. No ghostly carriage, no chilling manifestations, no sounds except the wind in the trees. Jack pulled his horse to the side when they reached the end and, anxious to get on with his long journey, Arthur merely waved his thanks and chivvied old Boxer into a trot.

He looked back for a moment just in time to see Jack disappearing into the lane and suddenly remembered that other coachman and realised how alike they looked. For some reason the thought disturbed him all the way to Norwich.

Long before he reached there, Daisy had come riderless out of the lane and clomped along the street and into the yard of the Swan. Daisy had been down, her knees were scraped and she was shaking. But there was no sign of hurt on Jack's body when they found him dead at the side of the lane. Only his eyes were staring and these they mercifully closed.

The Enigma of Ickworth Rectory

During those far-off peaceful years of the Edwardians and afterwards through the trials of the Great War, the parish church of Ickburgh in Norfolk flourished in the hands of the rector, the Rev. Cyril Mitford. Like many another old-style country parson, the rector had his little eccentricities, conceded to him as a right by the villagers by virtue of his superior education and place in local society. His appearance, for example, aroused some notice at a time when clerical garb was generally grey and sober, for he always dressed in a long black cassock and with a biretta sitting awry on his head. Tall and imposing, his was a figure familiar to all the natives of Ickburgh and around, as he was forever walking or riding the footpaths and lanes or on rare occasions driving off in his dog-cart towards Brandon. For newcomers he was the first person to be pointed out and for children a dignatory to incur awe and respect. Even the farming community allowed themselves a grudging admiration for the rector's concern for wild-life and his obvious grasp of agricultural matters – in his way a Kilvert of the Breckland.

The rector lived comfortably in the rather massive rectory close by the church with his childless young wife. As to how much the rector's eccentricities were displayed inside the rectory and indeed the whole story of their life together within those walls is, of course, impossible to know. Certainly the servant girls had tales to tell on their days off but so did servant girls everywhere and it amounted to no more than the usual tittle-tattle. Their mistress in particular suffered from very little criticism from anyone. She was not only engagingly good-looking but friendly and helpful, performing the required duties both as housewife and clergyman's help-mate with elegant good grace. Both husband and wife obviously made many sacrifices in the way of domestic comforts because of the compelling demands of pastoral care over a large village and the running of the big house was sadly dislocated on frequent occasions. The only reservation that Mrs. Mitford seems to have made was to be excused occasionally from attending morning service on Sundays since she considered it important to prepare a good lunch for the rector to sustain him through the heavy day.

When the Great War came, it shattered the age-old peace of Ickburgh as certainly as it affected stability everywhere. The sense of loss and of inevitable change was deeply impressed in the minds of the country folk. Because the crisis that occurred at the rectory came so close after the Armistice, it raises the first question of so many others in this strange story as to whether that sensitive period of aftermath had anything to do with the Mitford's personal affairs. Whatever contributed to the situation from outside there seems no doubt that there was little overt consideration of such an event from inside the rectory. When it happened, people were forced to wonder if the rector's obvious pride and pleasure in his beautiful wife had blinded him to the knowledge of what she was really like. That knowledge came to him suddenly one Sunday morning in

24

early 1919 and it was an experience so profound that it almost unhinged his mind and assuredly drove him to an early grave.

It was a short and pleasant walk to take from the church to the rectory after morning service was over. One can imagine that the rector would leave the concerns of church and religion temporarily behind him at that point and perhaps direct his thoughts towards the temporal blessing of a well-prepared Sunday lunch. On the day in question he reached the front door in the best of humour but was momentarily surprised that the door would not open. No doubt there was a good, house-wifely reason. He walked round to the back door. It was locked – all the doors and windows were locked. He stood in complete confusion for a few moments then went to window after window shouting his wife's name. There was no reply. He remembered that the servants were having their day off. The rectory was deserted.

More puzzled than alarmed at first, the rector accepted neighbourly help to get access into the house and he at once made for the kitchen where his wife would normally be busy with the meal. Alas, neither food nor wife was in evidence. Worse still, personal belongings that she would take if travelling had disappeared. It was a cruel and stunning blow. He stood like a man completely lost, as yet unable to accept the reality that his wife had gone, that she had left him for some unknown reason and for some unknown destination that he was never to discover.

Overnight the rector seemed to become a changed person. No longer striding along in his old, confident way, he appeared in the village as one weighed down by his distress. The gossips had their field-day and the church dignatories squeezed out a modicum of sympathy but no one realised how deep the wound had been. The rector was unable to continue with his work and soon became too depressed even to leave the rectory. In a few short weeks the once stout-hearted minister reached a point where he desired nothing but death to end his unhappiness. Indeed, this was soon granted to him and as the villagers gathered at the graveside to mourn such a tragic end, they had no doubt but that he had died of a broken heart.

While he was dying in his lonely bedroom, the rector could have had little thought for material matters, yet he managed to make a will and to list certain church treasures which had been hidden away during the Great War. At his request, a churchwarden attended at his bedside but found him very weak. It seemed that the rector recognised his visitor and appeared anxious to impart some sort of information to him but could do no more than move his lips in trying to say the words. For all his agitation, he could not be understood. Later, the church officials came to believe that he had been trying to speak of the listed treasures for some of these were never found. Had he placed them in some safe hiding-place that no one else knew? It was another mystery to add to that greater mystery of his wife's sudden disappearance.

Perhaps it was of this greater concern of his that the rector was trying to speak, a conclusion more likely indeed since it was this that obsessed his mind. But who can tell? All one can be sure about is that the rector's intense emotion during those last days caused his spirit to be rooted there in that room long after his death.

It was the new rector, the Rev. Barrett-Lennard, who first saw the ghost. He and his family had moved into the rectory after a decent interval during which a good deal of cleaning and refurbishing went on to suit their newer tastes. In the course of settling in, the new rector occupied the room where Mitford had died. On the very first night he was awakened suddenly to find a shadowy figure in the room. As his eyes became accustomed to the gloom he could make out quite clearly that the visitor was dressed in a long black cassock with a biretta on his head. Though showing no interest in the bed or its occupant, the figure seemed intent on some sort of search for it moved swiftly to and fro a few times and at intervals seemed to touch and inspect different parts of the wall. At one point the shadowy priest leaned forward and appeared to take something from the wall in a plucking motion. Then eventually the unhappy ghost returned to the fireplace where it seemed to disappear downwards into the floor.

Knowing the story of the missing church treasures, the Rev. Barrett-Lennard construed these actions as providing some sort of clue as to their whereabouts. Chimney, floors, wainscot – all were thoroughly investigated but revealed nothing. The theory that the ghost's apparent confusion could have been caused by the interior renovations was also considered but rejected. Practically no changes had been made in that particular room.

It was not until this line of thought was exhausted that those concerned accepted that the continued haunting was probably related to the poignant matter of the wife's disappearance. Was there some kind of message in the ghost's behaviour – an echo of that urgent attempt at communication made by the dying rector? Perhaps it was searching for a letter or a photograph? Or was the spirit simply being recalled time after time to the scene of the tragedy it could not forget?

For a long period after the Barrett-Lennards had settled in, the visitations continued at irregular intervals. The black-cassocked figure was seen most often by the rector himself but it was also seen by his wife and his son, whose descriptions tallied exactly. In time the family achieved a kind of humorous tolerance towards their nocturnal visitor, at least until that unhappy day when its presence claimed an innocent victim.

That day, by what mischance it happened one can only speculate, the family's dog was left in the room. Apparently it howled and scratched the door in a frenzy until let out but unfortunately it never recovered from the experience. It became rapidly mad and had to be destroyed.

As for the mysteries – the lost wife, the lost treasures – they never have been resolved.

Figures from the Past

I was a young girl of only eleven or twelve years old when this strange thing happened. It is so long ago that people may well ask how I remember so well but every detail of that day is as clear to me as if it were yesterday.

We lived then in Bury St. Edmunds and every Saturday afternoon my mother would take my sister and me for a walk into the country. Sometimes one of our aunts would come along with us. We used to walk about two miles, looking for wild flowers or leaves which we would take home to press for our collections.

The walk was always the same, starting from our house in Mustow Street, along Eastgate Street and on to the Great Barton road. We had to go under a railway arch along this road and this was a piece of our journey I did not like since the bridge was always so dark and lonely looking. Once through the arch, though, we were in more open country and we were able to run about or hunt around for flowers or feathers or whatever it was we were collecting at that particular time. When we got as far as a large pit that used to be beside the road we would usually decide that that was far enough and begin our walk back home.

One Saturday in October – it would be round about the twentieth of the month – we were just starting our journey back and Mother realised that it was getting colder and made us hurry along although we were all in coats and there was no wind at all. Soon the pit was left behind and I was anxious to get through the dreary railway arch and carry our few flowers home in good condition.

Then something happened which took our thoughts from such trivial things. On the right hand side of the road where we were walking there was just a wire fence and on the other side the ground fell away in quite a steep slope down to the fields so that what we saw was as clearly set out as if it were on a stage. Two figures had emerged from a distant field and were about to cross the field below us and we all stopped in surprise because it looked so strange. They were not ordinary people in winter clothes having a walk. They were both in white and were without any outer garments at all and they were stumbling along as if they were trying to hurry but could not make much progress.

The first thought that came into my young head was that they must be very cold without any outdoor clothes. Then I noticed that one of them was a lady wearing a long white nurse's uniform and that the head-dress and apron were billowing out as if in a strong wind though in fact the air was very still. The other figure was a man dressed in long white tight trousers and on his head he wore a small round black hat. It looked to me like a skull-cap but I have since wondered if it was not one of those military 'pill-boxes' worn long ago by some regiment of the army.

The two strange figures hobbled across the field with the nurse apparently helping the man along. They were clinging together and making laboured but very anxious progress. It looked as if they would reach the road not far ahead of us and just beside the railway bridge. My sister and I were for running ahead to get a close look at the couple but Mother made us stay by her side.

At the railway bridge the two white figures crossed the road and climbed the bank on the side that led upwards across a small field. They seemed very tired and only got up the bank with great difficulty, the man depending more and more on the nurse's help. The nurse's old-fashioned long uniform was often dragging in the mud. They did not look round or seem to think of anything but their own predicament, nor of anyone who might be watching.

Beyond the field that the two were crossing was a thick and neglected piece of woodland that we call the Glen. When we realised that they were going into the Glen it seemed so extraordinary that my sister and I wanted to follow them. Again my mother refused to allow us to do so and we continued walking home towards Eastgate Street feeling rather excited at the encounter.

In the clear picture I have of that afternoon's adventure I remember the contrast between those two figures engaged in some unknown drama and the ordinariness of everything else. The gathering dusk, leaves in the gutters, one or two people out walking, a car beside the road that wouldn't go and two impatient men trying to get it started. We had scarcely passed them by before we stopped again, because we seemed to have heard a scream coming from the direction of the Glen. Then there was a shot, quite clear to all of us, for Mother afterwards admitted that she had heard it too though at this point she seemed anxious to get us home as quickly as possible.

31

When we reached Mustow Street, my sister and I were in such a hurry to tell Grandma we tried to race each other into the house. Grandma was folding clothes that she had just ironed and she did not say a word until we had finished. Then she came and sat down with us beside the fire and put her hand on mine where it was resting in my lap.

"Were you frightened?" she asked. We said no, not really frightened, just excited and puzzled and somehow very sorry for the two people. What were they doing there, we wanted to know and what were they running away from?

"What you saw were not real people," Grandma told us quietly. "They were ghosts. And since you have seen so much and so clearly I think you should know the whole story." She looked at Mother for agreement and Mother nodded her consent. Then she went out of the room to put her hat and coat away and we two girls waited eagerly for Grandma to begin.

"That all happened a long time ago," Grandma told us, "well, you can judge for yourselves because I was only about your age when I was told the story and it was long before that when it actually happened. There was a hospital in Fornham Road then and at the time of the Crimean War a few of the wounded were brought there to be cared for. Of course you've heard of Florence Nightingale and how she had to fight to open the way for respectable young women to become nurses. Seems ridiculous now, but there was a lot of opposition to such advanced ideas and at the Fornham Road hospital very strict rules were laid down when two local girls volunteered to do nursing work there.

One of the girls was Mary Treese, who came from

a village not many miles away where her father was a farmer. Poor Mary, it was difficult for her. For one thing, her father strongly disapproved of the idea and there was prejudice and suspicion on all sides. Then there were the harrowing sights and experiences she encountered in the hospital and the strict discipline she had to follow. She was very young and very much alone. It is not surprising, really, that she and a young wounded soldier should become fast friends because they both needed the other's help and strength to survive. In a short time they became so much a part of each other's life that they could not think of parting.

Unfortunately, Mary and her young soldier, whose name I can't remember, couldn't disguise the fact that they were in love and that they met secretly whenever they could. I suppose their need for each other was greater than their fear of the consequences for they must have known how it would end. As soon as word reached the Matron, Mary was threatened with instant dismissal if the affair did not cease immediately. At the same time the army was informed that the soldier would be better in some other hospital.

Mary and her lover accepted the news quietly as if they were aware of but could not escape the unhappy destiny that their situation had forced upon them. They made no attempt to do other than be together at every possible moment. In a great temper at being disobeyed, the Matron sent for Mary's father, claiming that the girl had brought disgrace on the hospital and must be taken away at once. The farmer believed that the responsibility lay with the soldier and in a fury at what he thought was an attack on his daughter's honour, he went off to the hospital with a loaded shotgun in his hands. Almost at the same time an army unit arrived to take the soldier away.

Mary came to the young soldier's bedside when she realised that there was little hope of escape from the forces that were gathering about them, yet the thought of being separated was so painful to them both that they set off as they were, out of the back way and over the fields by the railway embankment. The soldier had a leg wound and could hardly move so that Mary had to help him along. I don't suppose they had any plan of what they were going to do. They just wanted to be with each other as long as possible. So they crossed the road just where you were watching today and went up to the wood to try and hide there.

Of course, it was quite hopeless. The army unit was already in the hospital and it would not take long for them to catch up. But even before that happened the farmer arrived following the directions of someone who had seen the couple enter the wood, and making no secret of his rage as he pursued them. In a small clearing he found them together under a tree, the soldier leaning against the trunk with a look of intense pain on his face and Mary stooping at his feet apparently tending his wound.

At the moment when Mary saw her father and the raised gun she screamed and began to run towards him but it was too late. He took a step to the side and fired point blank at the soldier's chest. When the army unit arrived they found that terrible tragedy – the soldier dead, the father waiting in a kind of daze to be taken as a murderer and poor Mary out of her mind with grief.

Well, that's the story. As you could see for yourselves, that forlorn little journey across the fields still happens on rare occasions because of all the pain and despair that existed there. One thing is certain – you'll never forget it as long as you live."

The Man in the Red Coat

About the last thing that can be observed in relation to ghostly experiences is any kind of pattern of behaviour. Nor is there a common denominator to which ghosts generally can be reduced although there is a loosely-held belief that they are inclined to appear in white. The shapeless body in a sheet fills the conventional idea of a ghost as near as anything though it is very doubtful if such a picture comes from anything outside the bounds of fiction. After all, white ghosts in dark rooms are a dramatic necessity but people with actual experiences to tell hardly ever mention anything so bizarre. Another piece of drama much admired by earlier writers was a manifestation at the witching hour of midnight. If there is any generalisation which can be made about ghosts it is that they tend to keep rather later hours nowadays – perhaps driven to it by the encroachment of radio and television – and one o'clock in the morning seems a more respectably modern time in which to be seen around. In the experiences of Mr. Arthur Wimslow, who lived for a time at Ditchingham in the Waveney valley area, the pregnant moment nearly always occurred at 1.30 a.m.

It was after a spell abroad that A.W. came to take a part of Ditchingham House, formerly the home of Lilias Rider Haggard whose grandfather, the distinguished author, lived in nearby Ditchingham Hall. He found himself in a fine old Georgian house with large

Elizabethan-type windows and it was in front of one of these that he often sat at his desk to work at night. The window was uncurtained and looked out on to the lawn. It was just at 1.30 on this particular night when he glanced up at the window, saw his own image clearly reflected in the glass and for a moment he gave no thought to the matter. Then he realised that there was something else beside his own reflection. As if standing immediately behind him and leaning slightly over his shoulder was the unmistakable figure of another man. The man was quite clearly wearing a red coat. In astonishment, A.W. slewed round in his chair to look at the newcomer but could see nothing. Thinking that perhaps he had been working too long and was beginning to see things that were not there, he decided this was probably a good time to give up work for the night. He went to bed and forgot all about the incident.

It was only a few days later that something happened to bring it back very vividly to his mind. He was entertaining a few friends in the most un-ghostly of circumstances, in fact in the full light of noon and with the cheerful noise of conversation going on all around. Some of the guests were standing, some of them sitting in the window-seat but all of them gathered before the same large window in which A.W. had seen the reflection. It is doubtful if any of them, least of all A.W. himself, had any thought of ghosts. Yet at the very moment of the greatest merriment a figure that was not of the group moved across the room in the direction of the open door which led to the main staircase descending to the floor below. Despite the blur of guests moving and talking there was no mistaking the extra man, for he was wearing a red coat. A.W. immediately made to follow as the man exited to the top of the staircase but in the few seconds delay he had disappeared.

From then on the man in the red coat occupied a good deal more of A.W.'s thoughts. What kind of a ghost would walk at midday in the midst of a crowd of people and what kind of man would wear a red coat anyway? Somehow, a huntsman's coat did not seem to fit the bill. More likely the coat of some Georgian dandy and if so what was the tale behind this long and ghostly sojourn in the old house? A.W. prepared himself for further visits from the apparition and watched particularly the sensitive area of the large window but for some time the unwanted visitor seemed to be lying low. Then suddenly there was the unforgettable night when the apartment seemed to explode with the sound of cries and screams.

It was just at 1.30 a.m. when the environs of Ditchingham House were at their sleepiest and when even the owls seemed to have joined the prevailing quiet, that pandemonium broke out in the guest room. In a moment A.W. was awake and rushing to the room where he found the guest, a level-headed young woman unused to making emotional scenes sitting up in bed and shaking with fear.

"What on earth is the matter?" demanded A.W.

"Look! Can't you see?" she screamed. "It's there. Look!"

A.W. could see nothing in that part of the room to which she was pointing but he did see something else. Quite clearly and slowly across the bedroom at about head height moved a small white cloud, a floating piece of ectoplasm that looked like a crumpled handkerchief. So far as A.W. was concerned it was strange but not to that degree frightening. He applied himself to seeking a rational explanation, and noting that the heavy window curtains were drawn and could not admit moonlight, viewed the handkerchief from all points. His guest, however, seemed unable to take the matter objectively and was clearly very frightened. She suddenly screamed again and in some sort of panic fell out of the bed heavily on to the floor. As soon as she was able to gather her limbs for flight she made for the bathroom where she locked herself in. It took a great deal of persuasion on A.W.'s part to induce her to emerge sometime later.

"Why didn't you tell me the place was haunted," she wanted to know. "It gave me the biggest shock of my life."

"What, that handkerchief thing. Yes, I saw that. I'm truly sorry it caused you such an upset."

"Not that, you idiot, though that was quite bad enough. Didn't you see him standing there when you came in?"

"Who? Standing where?" A.W. began to remember his earlier experiences in the house, which he had never mentioned to the girl.

"There was a man there wearing a red coat. And I felt – I was sure that he was there to kill somebody. When you came in I thought that it might be you because he had lifted a chair above his head and it looked as if – I think if I hadn't screamed and fallen out of bed he'd have hit you over the head with it."

As it happened, this was the last time that the man in the red coat appeared to A.W. or his friends but it does not complete the story of the manifestations at Ditchingham House. On an even more memorable night an apparition of quite another kind brought its attendant aura of horror and disbelief. By great misfortune it was the same young woman who experienced this event, at the identical time of 1.30 in the morning and in the same bedroom.

As on the other occasion, A.W. was awakened by a piercing scream from the direction of the room. When he entered he found her quite numb with fear, her hair stiff as if standing on end, her eyes staring at something in the room.

"Can't you see her?" she gasped in answer to A.W.'s solicitous questions. He looked around. He could see nothing. He tried to quieten the girl and persuaded her at last to go back to sleep. It was not until the next morning that he received a full and cogent account of what had happened. Even when remembering the incident, she started to shiver again.

"It was a woman," she said. "I woke up suddenly in the night and there was a woman beside me. I saw her very clearly – she had a kind face and grey hair. I woke up to find her stroking my hair on the pillow, stroking it slowly and gently. When I saw her I screamed and she backed away with a hurt look on her face. She was still there when you came in and she looked at you over her shoulder as she went to a spot over there and seemed to sit down. Only she sat down very low, almost on the floor. Then she disappeared."

Who was she? A.W. wondered. Was she associated in any way with the man in the red coat? Why was that room more particularly the scene of these ghostly appearances? In a moment of inspiration he sought the advice of the Rider Haggard family who were able to provide immediate illumination on the identity of the woman visitor though none at all on the red-coated gentleman. It seemed that the figure of the woman who stroked the girl's hair had some justification for being in that room for this was almost certainly Lilias Rider Haggard, the writer, who had used the room not only for sleeping but also for working at her desk. The desk had been standing just where the girl had seen her sit down. But why did she seem to sit so low down on that ghostly stage-set that night?

The answer gave the touch of authenticity to a tale which might have been disposed of as being some kind of nightmare. Some time after Lilias Rider Haggard's death, the floor had been raised to give some extra height to the room below. Where the ghost had sat down was exactly where she would have sat at her desk and exactly at the level at which she would have been sitting had the floor not been raised.

Bealings Bells

It was a Sunday afternoon of a kind fit to crown the glories of that long hot summer. Nothing moved, nothing disturbed the warm haze that carried the scent of roses and the soporific hum of insects in the village gardens. At Major Moor's house, the only two servants in residence that day walked out of doors and enjoyed the sun in leisurely fashion, no doubt recalling the excitements of the previous day when they had visited the travelling fair on the Common. Everyone in the house, except the master, had gone to the fair, even Cook herself between the demands of lunch and dinner and had walked the mile or so in good company along the sunlit lanes.

Today was quite a different story, of course, being Sunday with all its attendant requirements of modesty and decorum but nevertheless it was the garish attractions of the fair that lingered in the minds of the two servants through the unhurried hours. Although on duty, there was little for them to do since their master had gone out early to church and was likely to make a day of it, probably staying for lunch at one of his many friends and making a leisurely walk home in the late afternoon. For once the house was undemanding of their labour and both manservant and maid basked as long as they dared in the shimmering warmth of the garden. Then, in mid-afternoon they went into the house to change into more formal dress and to pre-

43

pare the Major's simple evening meal.

It was while they were in the kitchen, with nothing more serious in their minds than their sweethearts and their next day off, when one of them suddenly pointed to the wall where the bells were fixed. One of the bells, that which was normally activated from the dining room, was moving and jigging about. It was one of twelve attached to a board by springs and operated each by a wire from the main rooms. As the two servants watched, the dining-room bell began to ring – a sudden intrusion of noise in the quiet afternoon that shocked them into an automatic reaction to the bell's demands and the parlourmaid had actually taken a step toward the door before they remembered. There was no one in the house but themselves.

They had scarcely recovered from their consternation at the first ringing when it came again, a short but insistent summons that was followed a few minutes later by another. Unwilling to investigate the cause by themselves, the two servants waited with increasing apprehension for the return of their master. He was late. The dining-room bell stirred and rang again. As if mesmerised, they stared at the bell long after it had become silent again, expecting every moment that it would start once more. It was in some haste and with a touch of hysteria that they greeted the Major in his doorway, ready enough to pass the burden of the mystery over to him.

Major Moor, as it happened, was an ex-army man of considerable energy and resource, who normally dealt with problems with the confident analysis of a trained mind. In this case, however, his immediate impression was that the servants' nerves were on edge through having spent the day in the almost empty

44

house and were inclined to exaggerate whatever it was that had happened. Anyway, he decided, it was only something he could deal with if he were a witness. The matter was dismissed and the quiet and efficient routine of the house continued.

The Major was in his study during the next afternoon. Suddenly the same dining-room bell rang out again in the kitchen. The Major was brought to the scene and sure enough, after a short silence, the bell agitated itself and rang again, in all three or four times during the afternoon. The Major was puzzled, made a perfunctory examination of the bell system but, having other things on his mind at the time, merely promised to look further into the matter if it happened again.

Tuesday began bright and sunny but by noon there were threatening clouds building up and it seemed that the long spell of fine weather was about to break. There was an ominous look to the sky, something that led to considerable gloom in the servants' hall, especially when the Major decided that he would have to go out. He would be back, he assured them, by about five o'clock. No need to worry about the bells – he would see about it when he got back.

The cook and four other servants were in the kitchen finishing their lunch when the storm broke. Heavy, rumbling thunder followed the lightning flashes that intensified the gloom in the old house and there were sudden gasps from the younger girls as in the midst of it all the bell again rang out its enigmatic demand. It was a summons of some kind, it seemed to the servants, but a summons to whom and for what unimaginable reason?

But now, as the dining-room bell continued to ring,

another joined in, then another. Before the eyes of the frightened servants every bell of the twelve but one, which was broken, began to jig up and down and then to peal out in a deafening cacophony that made an insane accompaniment to the rumbling thunder.

At intervals the bells would stop but very soon one, or different combinations of bells would begin again with a maddening insistence. When the Major returned to the house at five o'clock he needed no hysterical servants to acquaint him with the events of the afternoon. The bells were jangling forth as he arrived. With his son beside him, he stood with the servants in the kitchen and shared their feelings of awe and impotence as he watched the bells, now ringing so violently that he thought they would be shaken from their fastenings. He noted that the five bells on the right of the board were always the most active but if there were but one ringing it would always be that of the dining-room. Intervals between the bouts of ringing seemed to last about a quarter of an hour and on this, the third day of the phenomenon, the performance continued with such time lapses until a quarter to eight in the evening.

The ceasing of the noise was as sudden as its onset and just as nerve-racking to the servant girls who worked in a daze and found their eyes constantly turning in a fearful fascination to the row of bells. Yet each session of ringing began so suddenly and violently that it always caused a gasp or a dropped utensil, followed by a kind of weakness of will caused by the sheer uncertainty of what was happening and what significance it had. It was high time that the Major applied himself to the solving of the problem before his staff had hysterics and left.

So, in fact, the good major busied himself in one way or another, reducing all the possibilities he could think of for the cause of this strange and noisy invasion of his house. His particular training and experience persuaded him to work on the assumption that there must be a logical and probably a physical, reason. He soon dismissed the suggestion that mice could be suspect but spent more thought on the idea that a very small boy of nimble mind and body could often wreak a quite disproportionate amount of havoc. However, the only small boy with access to the rooms was his grandson and the major determined to have him at his side during any further demonstrations.

So comprehensive were the major's efforts that the household woke up on Wednesday morning with some confidence that he had somehow managed to still the hand that could pull the bell wires from a dozen different rooms at once. Such faith buoyed up the spirits of the servants but they could not help noticing that their master himself seemed far from happy about the situation. In fact, he had been unable to find any sensible cause for the bells to ring and so resolved that since he could do no more by practical means he would at least ensure that any further manifestation would be properly witnessed and attested for the benefit of scoffers and sceptics.

Accordingly, he gathered in the kitchen an impressive number of interested individuals including his son, his grandson, all the servants, a newspaper reporter and an errand boy on his rounds. The major had locked all the doors, covered the bell-pulls within the rooms, dismissed all pets, examined the bells and the wall behind them minutely in company with others. All they could do now was to wait for a recurrence of

47

yesterday's experiences. Perhaps there was a smile on the face of a newcomer to the vigil thinking what an odd occupation it was for about ten sane people on a summer's morning to be watching a row of bells on a kitchen wall.

Such a smile would be short-lived. Suddenly one of the girls screamed, her nerves taut with expectancy. The dining-room bell was moving; it was shaking. It was ringing. Another and another bell chimed in until all those on the right hand side of the board were ringing violently. Then they all stopped. There was an interval of three or four minutes before the bells jangled out again. In various permutations all the eleven bells sounded with increasing clamour and it was the wildness of the ringing that awed the watchers, the bells leaping furiously in the air so that one actually touched the ceiling. The ringing was intermittent, with pauses so silent it seemed as significant as the noise itself and during which many of those present could hear their own hearts beating. None of those present could help but feel, each time that the bells jangled forth, that the whole performance was associated with some power beyond earthly knowledge.

The ringing went on, without pattern or sense, well into the evening and after most of the visitors had gone and the major was left with no comfort to give to the servants nor any solution to ease his mind. All the ingenuity and applied logic of the army man had achieved nothing. He recalled the outburst of a distraught servant during one of the intervals of silence: "What do they want, whoever it is? What do they want from us?"

Did someone want something? Could it be that this was some kind of communication from someone outside the human sphere who needed their attention? Who could tell? Humbled and disturbed, the major watched the bells until midnight and then retired.

As if it was this spiritual capitulation by the major that was required by the mysterious bell-pullers or because some occult design had been satisfied that day by the overwhelming demonstration of its power, such a frantic clamour was never to occur again. The ringing became more casual, less insistent and in time reverted to the original single dining-room bell. In a few weeks they were heard no more.

"A pointless bit of campanology," wrote some critic, leading the flood of scepticism that followed the inevitable publicity. Even Bernard Barton, the Woodbridge poet, felt himself moved to write a longish poem in the same mood of good-humoured raillery.

But it was not pointless, that strange and noisy exercise in communication. No one in that house would be the same again, not so certain, not so earthbound. From that time on they would be unable to shield themselves with disbelief or laugh at the things they did not understand. Like it or not, they had been initiated into some new concept, something outside their normal consciousness and it would remain with them to the end of their days.

Murder at High House

From looking at the stories of ghosts that manifest themselves in large and lonely country houses, it seems certain that wicked squires really did exist in the manner and number of those portrayed in Victorian fiction. Derisive though we may be of such bygone melodrama, there was a good deal in it that was very near to the truth. Cold records as well legend show that the moustache-twirling, riding-booted bigwig was often as beastly as his reputation. If he was not turning poor old folk out of their homes into the snow at frequent intervals he was probably saying "What ho, me proud beauty," to some young woman caught in the unfortunate dilemma of losing her honour or paying the rent.

A further disreputable tendency among the downright wicked squires was to turn up again in spirit form while self-congratulatory smiles were still showing on the faces of the bereaved. At Oulton High House, for example, the erstwhile master not only haunted the grounds there with great success for many years but managed to keep his pack of ghostly foxhounds with him.

It was the presence of the hunting dogs, perhaps, that aided the general belief that the squire's ghost seemed to be searching for something or someone. Those few people who claimed that they had seen him felt that he was trying to hunt out some secret from his past life. His appearances were rare, however, and usually the ghostly hunt began from and disappeared into the drooping branches of the ancient cedar.

The whole affair was wrapped in mystery until a Mrs. Zilla Thompson, hot-foot from a spiritual seance in Yarmouth, arrived as a guest at exactly the right moment to confront the huntsman in full tally-ho on the lawns. He immediately retreated to the shadowy base of the cedar and vanished. Mrs. Thompson used her considerable experiences in the supernatural together with a touch of intuition to decide that the dead squire was in fact searching for his wife, who had been responsible for some dastardly deed during her lifetime.

She was relating these conclusions to the lady of the house when the latter said: "Oh, of course, his wife! That must be the lady in white. We've seen her several times in the house. We call her Lady Macbeth. She always seems to have a purpose, always moving swiftly and silently, never still. Of course, we only see her for a few seconds. But there was one occasion when I saw her very clearly in the main corridor. She passed by quite close and she seemed to be carrying something in her hands – it looked like a cup."

"A cup!" exclaimed Mrs. Thompson, "then she was probably a poisoner."

She then engaged in an intense investigation of the whole affair, fascinated as she was by the incidence of two ghosts, both searching and unhappy, in the same house. That they had been husband and wife she felt certain; that they had been guilty of violent crimes to each other or to innocent people she strongly suspected. Some strange quest that would not let them sleep brought them both back to High House, only to be separated by irreconcilable forces, unknowing of each other.

What was the power that brought them, each apparently in search of the other? Some great love that would not die? Or guilt – or revenge? Mrs. Thompson set out to find the whole background of the couple's life at High House and as it was revealed, she wrote it down in meticulous notes and observations that came into the possession of her family when she died. It is from these guide lines that I have reconstructed the full story of the living couple and the violence wherein lies the cause of their restless haunting. Unfortunately, Mrs. Thompson gives no names in her notes on the main characters and so they remain simply the squire, his wife and their daughter.

There is no doubt that the squire was a man of a bigoted and oppressive nature, looked on with more awe than affection by his friends and with hate and distrust by many of those employed on his farms. Everyone who had dealings with him knew that he had a sudden and virulent temper and it was a trait he made no attempt to disguise when in the family home. In the early years of their marriage such outbursts of rage and jealousy were often directed at his wife. It is possible that in the course of time the effect would be to harden her resistance to such treatment to the point where she began to feel only hatred and contempt for her husband. With her loyalty destroyed by his suspicions, she eventually felt no compunction about deceiving him. This she did with several lovers in clandestine meetings or at the High House during her husband's regular absences.

A guest at the house at that time was a young Army officer on leave from the Hussars and the object of growing suspicion on the part of the squire. There came a day when his jealousy was aroused to the point of making an unexpected re-appearance at High House when he was supposed to be far away at a foxhunt. He did indeed find his wife in the arms of the officer and forthwith set upon him with his riding crop, using all the venom of which his nature was capable. Seeing that it was a choice of using desperate measures or being battered to death, the officer dragged his sword from its scabbard and plunged it into the squire's heart.

There was nothing that the couple could think of then than to pack a few things and run. The officer had a house in rural Leicestershire to which they fled and hid until a few weeks later when he was apprehended and sent for trial. The squire's wife, placed beyond suspicion by her social station and by the officer's gallantry, continued to live in her new home until other repercussions from the past began to trouble her existence.

These repercussions were created by the fact that in her need to escape quickly from High House she had left behind her only child, her daughter. At that time about ten years old, the little girl would come to no harm through being abandoned by her mother since she would be well cared for by relatives and servants. So, in fact, she continued to live at High House until she grew up. In due course she learned of the crime and the cause of her lonely existence and became bitterly antagonistic towards her mother for the role she had played. No doubt there was some occasional communication between the two after the girl had reached the years of discretion but their relationship became increasingly acrimonious. When eventually the mother indicated that she wished to return to High

House, her daughter adamantly refused. She was now supported in her attitude by a young suitor who could see no good in having the mother in residence.

The daughter was by now about twenty years of age, rather headstrong like her father and determined that her mother should not upset what had become a comfortable and enjoyable way of life at High House. Nevertheless, just as obstinate, the mother persisted. She was not at all happy in Leicestershire. All her interests and all her personal belongings were still at High House and she intended to return. If she attempted to do so, the daughter replied, she would make public the part that her mother had played in the murder. Such was the intransigence of either side that there seemed to be no possible civilised solution and indeed led to the last grisly chapter in this story of violence.

One day when nothing seemed likely to disturb the peace of High House and the well-being of its occupants, the main door was thrown open and masked men entered. Pushing the servants aside, the men found the daughter at her embroidery in the drawing room. At her side was the young man to whom she was betrothed. In the hurried scuffle to seize the girl the young man attempted to defend her and was stabbed to death.

Once outside, the girl was bundled into a dark, hearse-like carriage and the horses were whipped up. There was a diminishing thunder of hooves and heavy wheels as the watchers from the house saw the strange conveyance disappear. Hours later it arrived at the mother's home and the girl was hastily ushered inside by the masked men.

What took place between mother and daughter at

the initial meeting can only be imagined. Certainly there was nothing of affection to soften the confrontation. Rather would there be heavy recrimination, blame and abuse from both sides in which neither would be prepared to compromise. If the mother had hoped for some concession from her daughter in the line of filial duty or through her own dominance of will, she was mistaken. For a few days the mother held her daughter in the house as a prisoner but the girl remained firm and it was in final desperation at the impasse she had brought on herself that the mother prepared the fatal poison. During the evening, the poisoned cup was handed to the girl who innocently drank it and died soon after.

All this and more Mrs. Zilla Thompson unearthed about the unhappy family at High House. Perhaps it was that she dug too deep into the mysteries for her notes show a growing disquiet. "It may be that I have been too assiduous in my researches," she wrote towards the end, "for I seem to have provoked a resistance of some kind from the spirit world which may well become active. However, I think that if I give up now and disturb them no more all will be well."

Whatever it was that Mrs. Thompson feared, it soon showed itself to be real. She died in mystifying circumstances only a few months later. She had been poisoned and by her bedside stood the fatal cup – a cup that no one knew within the house and which only those who had met the ghost at Oulton High House would be able to recognise.

Footsteps in the Dark

It began with no more than a suspicion of something strange in the atmosphere of the old house, a feeling so slight that it occasioned no concern at all in the new occupant's busy life. There had been no hint of anything untoward. No one had come forward to volunteer the information that the place was haunted and that whole generations of local people had been scared of walking past the house. Even if they had it is doubtful if it would have made any difference. Peter Broom knew it was the very kind of house he wanted and would enjoy living in – old and rambling, with many a nook and cranny and all the charms of its Tudor origins. There was a Victorian addition, to be sure, but when Peter set to work on renovations in preparation for his marriage it was on the fascinating Tudor part that he concentrated.

For some considerable time Peter worked and lived alone in the house and was not surprised that it was inclined to groan and creak sometimes, what with its ancient timbers and draughty doors. Being young and rational in outlook, he was usually able to associate unexpected noises with such things as broken shutters, branches beating against the windows or birds rustling in the eaves. Not everything, however, could be so simply explained and many a night would find him searching around outdoors with a lantern to seek some further cause. Perhaps, it he had known of the house's ghostly reputation he might have accepted the invasive noises as a hint that it resented a new tenant and was warning him off. As it was, Peter allowed no such fancies to deter him.

Unfortunately, other things began to happen. He was sitting in his office in the house one evening when the room became cold, so suddenly and distinctly that he rose from his chair with a very uneasy feeling. His dog, too, was alert and obviously disturbed. After a time the clammy feeling diminished, the tension passed, and man and dog went off once more on a tour of the house to try to find some reason for the strange experience.

As time went on, such incidents happened more frequently but the excitement of preparing what was otherwise an attractive old house for his forthcoming wedding allowed Peter to dismiss such matters from his mind. Until her own startling initiation into the hidden mysteries of the house, his fiancee knew nothing of the odd things that had been happening.

It was one Saturday evening, when his wife-to-be had come to the house to measure the windows for curtains and Peter was busy in another room. Suddenly she gave a loud scream and he rushed across the hall to find her cowering on the stairs. Something very frightening had occurred, she told him. The atmosphere had become suddenly very cold and something that she could not describe had brushed across her face. As he comforted her, Peter admitted his own experiences of a similar kind. It was a critical moment in their relationship. There was so much to love in the old house and yet so much to fear. Perhaps as her first reaction the young woman would have chosen to leave the place forthwith and forget the incident but, happily, further consideration and a good deal more discussion persuaded her to agree to soldier on, provided that such manifestations were not utterly malevolent. Such was their pluck and persistance that the couple stayed in the house, while suffering considerable attention from the resident ghost, for fourteen years.

At night there were footsteps in the house – footsteps that could be followed progressively along the passages, on the stairs and in the rooms above. It was with some misgiving that the new wife invited her mother to stay for a week-end some two months after the marriage. She was put into what was considered to be the least haunted room and after a tiring day all retired to bed in good time. It turned out to be a bad night for the visitor. People seemed to be walking about at all hours, with doors shutting just as she was getting off to sleep. It must be, she decided, that someone had been taken ill. Early next morning she came down full of anxious enquiries but received very vague and off-putting replies from the young couple. The fact that neither of them had left their room during the night was very difficult to explain without frightening their visitor out of her wits.

The footsteps, the unaccountable noises, the sudden changes of temperature and the acute uneasiness sometimes shown by their faithful old dog were phenomena that Peter and his wife learned to live with. What they were not prepared for was the development of more active, poltergeistic type of happenings as if a resentful presence was intensifying its campaign to get rid of them. However much they tried to explain it away the fact became evident that odd things happened to objects left lying around overnight. Such things as playing card packs were often moved from one place to another, sometimes disappeared altogether only to turn up again in a most unlikely situation a few days later. Ornaments were changed around or vanished out of sight to the most inappropriate hiding places. The candles that were placed at strategic corners in the old house to light a difficult step or some other hazard in the dark would often be found to have been extinguished, sometimes removed entirely. One morning when Peter came downstairs he found on the carpet in the hall a piece of copper wire two metres long. This was the crowning mystery of all for there was no known person who could have put it there nor was there any such wire anywhere around, indoors or out.

For all this, the couple endeavoured to follow a normal routine and confidently invited a number of guests for a kind of house-warming party some few weeks after they had moved in. It was worth the risk, they decided and unless there was something new or violent demonstrated by the resident spirits, all should be well. So indeed it was, until during the party a male visitor went upstairs to the bathroom. His lengthy absence was unnoticed by most of those present but not by his wife who came across to Peter in some concern and asked him to investigate.

Peter immediately did so and was able to witness the latest and most astonishing trick by the poltergeist. As he reached the top of the stairs he could hear a stream of curses interspersed with calls for help. Obviously the guest was somehow trapped in the bathroom but Peter could see from the far end of the landing that in fact the door was not shut. There was a gap of a few inches between the door and the frame, a gap that slightly increased and decreased in a series of jerks in the way that it would if two people of similar strength were pulling on opposite sides of the door. Nevertheless, there was no one visible outside the bathroom door and the prisoner inside seemed to be pulling against the empty air.

Unaware of this, and believing himself to be the victim of some practical joker, the beleaguered guest was becoming more and more indignant. Such phrases as: "Let go of the door, you bloody idiot," came to Peter's ears as he approached. When he was within a few feet of the door, the unknown force that had held it firm relinquished its hold and the door swung open quite easily.

"Some fool," complained the man, stumbling angrily on to the landing, "some fool has been holding the door shut." Peter examined the door. It opened and closed, as indeed it had always done, with complete smoothness.

By now, Peter and his wife had taken some measure of the ghost's capabilities and were no longer surprised when, for example, having heard the daily help from the village come in and enter the kitchen with all the appropriate sounds of arrival, their calls of greeting would go unanswered, the kitchen would be found to be empty and a few minutes later the real lady help would turn up.

After this had happened a few times, Peter began to wonder if there was a way in which he could confront the mysterious but far from silent presence in the house and perhaps obviate the gratuitous sound of footsteps. But how could it be done and where? Simply by matching the ghost's persistent activities with a stubborn human will? What, if anything, would impress on their invisible tormentor that nothing it could do would every drive them away? The only thing that Peter could think of was to make a stand in the path of the footsteps and see what happened. As the footsteps were often heard on the landing, that seemed to be the appropriate place for a confrontation.

He consulted his wife on the idea and found that she was at first unwilling because she considered that it could be dangerous. However, as time went on and Peter seemed more and more determined on the project, she agreed to assist.

On the day chosen, at what was considered to be the optimum time for the ghost to be walking, they both waited for a sign of its presence. Sure enough, in advance of the arrival of the daily help, there were the sounds of the false arrival, with noises in the kitchen and then on the stairs. Peter went up by the main staircase and stationed himself at one end of the landing while his wife took her place at the other end. It was not long before the footsteps began again on the landing. They were distinct, methodical steps moving in the direction of Peter's station. Judging the sound of the footsteps, he placed himself directly in their path. Nearer and nearer they came until he could feel the cold air gathering about him. Still he would not stir. Immediately in front of him and within a bare three feet, the footsteps ceased. Whatever it was, it stayed there until Peter leaned forward to stretch out his hands. He could feel only the clammy coldness. There was nothing else but at least the footsteps had been stopped, for the time being.

The couple saw the incident as a complete triumph. In future they would match aggressive tactics with their own confident rebuffs and even if they could never claim a complete victory, they no longer had any fear of what the enemy might do. The days of ghostly intimidation were over.

The Wild Man of Orford

"He's back!" said the fisherman – or thirteenth century words to that effect – as he threw a rope around a bollard on the quay at Orford. Skipper of the newly arrived smack being tied up, he seemed to find little pleasure in the remark. Nor did the handful of men standing on the quay exhibit any signs of unalloyed joy on hearing the information.

"What! Him?" asked one, in the best tradition of monosyllabic Suffolk.

"Him," nodded the skipper. "Him agin and no one else. And caught up in the nets just as he was in the first place. He's shut up down below but he can't stay there long."

"I thought we'd done with him," offered another bystander nervously. "I felt a lot easier when he was out there in the bay."

"What should I do? Tell the Governor?" asked the fisherman spotting the town reeve among the others.

The reeve shook his head. "One thing," he said importantly "is the Governor ain't at home. Another is I reckon he was as glad to see that monster go as we all was. That won't please him at all to come back and find we'd captured the Wild Man all over agin."

"Take him out agin, Jack," advised the nervous man. "You'll be a-goin' out tomorrer with the boat. Take him as far as you go and jest drop him over the side."

"That seem the only thing I can do," sighed the skipper. "Take him out and try and lose him agin."

The assembled quay-side wise-acres nodded soberly. The Wild Man was no longer the subject of the intense interest that he once was and now that the Governor had washed his hands of him he had become something of an embarrassment and the best that could be proposed was that he should be returned to the deep.

Such a conversation, give or take a few oaths and expressions current at the time, might have taken place at any one of the several re-appearances of the Wild Man. The accounts of such matters and of all the strange business that surrounded this phenomenon from the sea were set down long ago by Ralph de Coggeshall, whose reputation as a meticulous chronicler earned him a credibility that far outlasted his lifetime and ensured that the story would be handed down through the ages as originally recorded. It began when the Wild Man was first caught in the nets of an Orford fishing boat in 1204, trawled up with the fish from the mysterious depths.

On that occasion the excitement on the quay was intense. Reports of the creature's size and appearance, exaggerated minute by minute by the usual gossips, brought the villagers flocking to the scene. It was a man all right, they discovered when he had been released from the net and safely secured, a man with most of the characteristics of any human, standing upright and apparently docile. What showed him also to be some kind of monster and immediately gave him the title of Wild Man was that he was completely covered in long black hair in place of clothes. He might have looked like some great shambling bear but that his head was entirely bald.

With their initial astonishment over, the fishermen and attendant villagers lost no time in informing the Governor at the Castle and followed the message by forming a large mob which gradually persuaded the shambling beast to walk in the right direction. In an hour they were at the Castle where the Governor came out and showed great interest in the Wild Man. He stood, still wet and sea-weed-draped, but apparently in no great discomfort at finding himself in a new element, except that in moving he shuffled along rather awkwardly. He seemed very curious about his surroundings and about the people who were standing around gaping at him but all in all he behaved in a totally docile and tractable manner.

The Governor was fascinated. The Wild Man was taken in to the Castle, adequately secured to begin with, but as the Governor learned more about the creature he gradually gave him more freedom. The Wild Man showed no violence nor any wish to leave. He fed entirely on fish and meat and was given a special long couch to sleep on. In a few weeks he had the right to roam the Castle so far as the Governor was concerned but this was a development not entirely to the liking of the soldiers and the servants there.

Unfortunately, the Wild Man had no kind of speech nor any means of communication with the humans. It was something that somehow incensed the menials in the Castle since they regarded his dumbness to be of an unnatural and possibly evil origin while there was also a suspicion that he could speak if he was made to.

It was during one of the Governor's absences from the Castle that resentment over the Wild Man came to a head. While they were bound to yield to the Governor's wishes in pampering the Wild Man when he was there, the servants refused to give precedence to the dumb creature when he was not. They tried to provoke him by withholding food, by putting him in a dungeon for a spell and by striking him whenever he was asked a question and did not answer. At the climax of this animosity the Wild Man was taken out, secured in the Castle courtyard and beaten.

When the Governor returned he displayed rather more humane ideas about achieving responses from his unusual guest. Most notable of these was the experiment in taking him to Mass in the parish church at Orford. One Sunday morning when the parishioners were already assembled, the great door opened to admit the Governor. Behind him was the shambling ape-man who followed the Governor abjectly to his seat.

If the Governor expected that the Wild Man would be somehow impressed by the civilising influence of the ceremony, he and no doubt the clergy present were to be disappointed. The Wild Man was vastly curious for a few minutes but seemed to tire of the intoning priest and seeing no point in his own creature mind why he should be detained there, shuffled out. Servants took him back to the Castle. Perhaps it was at this time that the Governor himself began to lose interest in his prodigy. What had been a marvel to him and his friends for a limited period now became a bit of a bore. There was not much future in the entertainment value of a creature that just wanted to eat and sleep in feudal comfort.

The idea of netting off a portion of the river occurred to him; there the Wild Man would be in the element in which he naturally belonged and still available for observation. The project was certainly welcomed by the townsfolk who had felt more than a little uneasy at the presence of the monster. The Wild Man was returned to the waters beside the quay where many a villein came to gape and wonder at such a fish. Then suddenly he was gone. He had found a gap in the netting and escaped into the sea. The Governor was not unduly concerned. There were very few things you could do with a dumb Wild Man once the novelty had worn off.

How many times the Wild Man re-appeared on the quay at Orford, in the village itself or in the grounds of the Castle, it is impossible to say. He had become so much a part of the legend of the place that his comings and goings existed more often in the imaginings of superstitious villagers, some of whom would use the threat of the Wild Man for purposes of their own, than in actual fact. Certainly he turned up from time to time and once in the nets of the fishermen but there was no response to his coming from the Castle. After a long absence he was spotted by returning fishermen one evening as they passed by Dunwich cliffs. The Wild Man was standing there clear and alone and for more than the hour that he was within sight he did not move. He was not seen again.

Death by Terror

There is no doubt that a ghost story requires an appropriate time and place for its telling. It will wait at the back of your mind during morning light and mid-day activities but come evening or a late afternoon on a gloom-ridden autumn day and the shadows will remind you of strange and unexplicable things.

Such a time and place occurred when a group of building workers happened to be working in a village not far from Cavendish in the west of Suffolk. Because of the deteriorating weather, some of the men had taken shelter under the trees of a small wood there. Within sight was a lonely manor house, isolated enough in daylight but as the afternoon's shadows crept across the landscape it seemed to become menacingly dark and forbidding. No lights came on to give a friendly aspect to the place and the windows glowered sightlessly towards the woods. It was not difficult to imagine, as others often imagine, that hideous faces peered out from those windows into the darkness.

"That properly give me the creeps, the owd place," said one of the men, deliberately turning his back on the house and lighting a cigarette. The weather had become worse, sharp gusts of cold wind sweeping through the undergrowth while high above a veritable gale roared and swayed in the top branches of the trees. It became darker, the old house even more

71

desolate looking.

"I reckon that's haunted right enough," concluded another. "At least I shouldn't care to stay inside there on a dark night to find out."

"Haunted?" laughed a younger member of the group. "Blast, ghosts don't exist 'cept in peoples' hids. That wouldn't spoil my sleep to spend a night in there, any time."

"Hold you hard there, young 'un," interposed someone huddling close to the bole of a tree for shelter. "Don't you start being too cocksure. I seen people like you afore – too full of themselves to know what's good for them."

"What – d'you think there's ghosts, then?"

"What I think is about young men what boast. That take me back at least twenty year to the time when I knew another young chap and he was just as brave as you but that didn't keep him alive very long."

"What happened then?"

"Well, that started in just the same way as you was boasting just now. Far as I remember, exactly the same words. He'd spend a night in a haunted house and wouldn't mind a bit. That's what he told us and we was silly enough to let him do it. Been on my mind ever since. That's why I'm ticking you off for saying the same thing. I wouldn't want what happened to him to happen again to anybody."

"You ain't ever mentioned this afore," somebody said. "Are you sure you ain't just making it up?"

"I've hardly ever mentioned it afore mostly because that don't come to my mind. For one thing that happened a long time ago and another is you don't tend to think of such things in broad daylight. But something dreadful happened that night – something

almost beyond belief. I don't think I've ever told anyone the full story – but if you care to hear about it while
we're sheltering here I'll tell you all that I can remember."

"Yes," he went on, "that was just such a house as you
see here, an old Georgian manor-house set in a big
park but of course some distance away from here. It
stood about a mile outside the village where I used to
live and the people round about, they all reckoned it
was haunted. When we was kids we grew up to know
all the tales about the place and we always reckoned we
could see somebody's face at the window, though the
house had been empty and abandoned for many a
year. The main story about the house – well, I can't re-
call the details but that concerned a certain bedroom.
We used to point out which winder it was but we das-
sen't go too near. They said it was that room and what
had happened there that drove out the owners and
they never came back.

Well, I was a young man then, one of the village lads
who used to patronise the local pub of an evening. We
was a little group of mates, like, feeling a bit big at
drinking more than was good for us and not old
enough to know that beer may be good for boosting
up your spirits but no damn good at all for your wits.

The night that I'm talking about, that was about the
same time o' the year as this, I remember and there was
a good old fire in the bar and we boys – well, men as
we thought ourselves – we sat around nice and warm
and somebody brought up the subject of ghosts. Well,
speak of ghosts in that neighbourhood and you were
bound to come up with something about the old
haunted house.

I don't recollect exactly how that happened but everyone was getting a bit braver the nearer he got to the bottom of his glass and very soon young Martin Webcoat, who was a farmer's son and as full of devilry as anyone around there, he was boasting that he wouldn't be afraid to go up to the old manor house at night and into the haunted bedroom too, come to that.

"Anyone want to come with me?" he asked us. No one did. Talking about ghosts beside a good fire was a different thing to actually going up to the old house after dark. "Well, I'm going," he said, "and there ain't no better time than the present."

We others, we was of the age when everything is a bit of a joke so we kind of egged old Martin on when we should have been trying to talk him out of it. When the landlord came round with some more drinks and heard what Martin meant to do, he couldn't wait to offer a wager that he would never go into the haunted room alone.

Of course that only made Martin more determined to go. Then someone with a bit of commonsense surviving in his addled mind asked: "If he do go up to the old manor house how could we ever know whether he's actually been into the haunted bedroom?"

"Tell you what," said the landlord, "if he's still dead set on going through with this I know a way we can prove it. That's simple enough. All he's got to do is to take a hammer and a nail and knock that nail into the bedroom door on the inside. If we go along the next morning and find the nail in place that'll be proof enough and I'll hand over my wager and welcome."

We was all pretty merry by closing time. No one would have cared a mite if Martin had given up the crazy idea and come on home with the rest of us. But he was too bull-headed to back down. When the rest of us set off along the road towards our comfortable beds, Martin was already clumping along through the meadow towards the old house. That was the last we see of him alive.

Make me wonder still when I think about it – about what happened to Martin when he reached the house. Knowing the sort of chap he was, he probably blundered straight in the front door carrying his hammer and a small torch the landlord had given him. But once inside – what was there? How can anyone tell what he met there in the hall or what was waiting there on the stairs in the dust and the quiet? There would be a little moonlight coming in through the winders but it must have made the place seem even more ghostly. When he had mounted the stairs he had to walk a little way along the landing and open the door of the haunted room and this we know he did, though what he met there in the gloom, what evil presences came out of the darkness we shall never know. The old house was brought down years ago.

That night, of course, we had no idea what had happened. Next day was Sunday and we youngsters were not feeling all that bright nor giving much thought to our drinking of the night before till nearly half-way through the morning. Then we see Martin's sister come along the road and she knocked on the door to ask if anyone had seen Martin and if anyone knew why he hadn't been home all night.

That struck us young chaps then what a serious sort of thing we'd been party to. We all ran along to the old manor house as quick as we could. There was about half-a-dozen of us, with Martin's sister and the landlord and the constable who we picked up on the way. We went inside that evil place and even in broad daylight and with other people around it sent shivers down your spine to climb those mouldering, rat-eaten stairs to the bedroom.

The constable went first or rather we probably pushed him ahead of us like but we all crowded round when he stopped at the half-open door of the haunted room. Martin was there sure enough, just inside the door in a grotesque sort of position. He was half-sitting, half-lying there alone and a look of utter terror on his face. He was dead right enough and had probably been dead almost from the moment that he opened the door.

Later on, when we'd recovered from the fright, we were able to piece together just what had happened. It was like this. When Martin arrived and climbed those rickety old stairs – and heaven knows what state of nerves he must have been in by that time – he saw the door of the haunted room along the landing and got ready the hammer and the nail that he was going to knock into the door. Dead scared as he was, he didn't want to go right into that room if he could help it and decided that, if he partly opened the door and reached round he could knock in the nail without irrevocably entering the room and closing the door behind him.

So, a little unsteady, a little bit hampered by his great-coat and scarf, he stretched round the half-open door and managed to knock the nail, with many a mishit in the dim light, and leave it well and truly bedded in the wood. All he wanted to do now was to get out of that awful house as quickly as he could.

But he couldn't move. He was standing just inside the door. The door was open but he could not move. He felt himself being held from behind – some fiend

76

with an iron hand refused to release him from that room. It must have come to him again, that old curse, repeated often enough when he was young, that if you were ever foolish enough to enter that room, you were unlikely to leave it again alive. Pull as he might in his increasing panic and sense of impending doom but the devilish forces chained him, holding him there in the room as if he were caught in a trap.

How long he lived in that terror that came upon him we don't know but the time came when his heart could stand the strain no longer and he collapsed. He fell in that awkward position we found him in because in the dark he had nailed his own coat to the door and it half supported him still. It seems that it was the nail that held him back, he being too stupid with drink and fear to realise it. It was the nail that held him. But it was the fiends in the room that drove him mad and killed him."

Robert and Mary

This ghost will not disturb your sleep – more likely that you would unwittingly disturb him yourself, unless you walk very quietly where he frequents. Beyond the river bridge at Melton, where the Deben channel narrows and the reeds nod and sigh together he has his tireless walk and a few have seen him there in the misty evening light. He is no shrouded spectre but a recognisably young man clothed in the simple garb of a countryman of over a century and a half ago. He does not stir often from the lonely water's edge but moves restlessly there as if absorbed in a search of his own cor.cern. A contagion of despair that accompanies his movements communicates itself at once to any who happen to glimpse this unhappy ghost.

One early morning, a villager sitting quiet and alone among the sedges with his rod and line, saw the figure as clearly as if he were of substance and took him in fact to be a fellow fisherman until he saw the trouble and anxiety in the countenance. "Are you lost?" he called out but the apparition passed swiftly by apparently in a daze of self-absorption until he dwindled and vanished among the clumps of reeds. The fisherman did not feel any fright at the encounter. In fact, as he confessed afterwards, he felt somewhat apologetic that his trivial occupation had impinged on some emotional plane in which he was merely an interloper.

The sad ghost's name was Robert Manly when he

lived and he was born and bred in the village of
Bromeswell, Suffolk, at about the time when, not far
away, the Martello towers were being built along the
coast against the threat of Napoleon's coming. As to
what kind of boy he was, it can only be judged by his
subsequent deeds but one can guess that he was a normal, quiet country lad, fearing God and the squire and
with a vidid interest in the wildlife and the farming activities of the immediate area.

Robert fell in love quite early on with a comely girl
of the same village named Mary King and like many
country love affairs their courtship took its untroubled
course over a number of years. There was never a
doubt in either of their minds as to the love and devotion which each felt for the other and which only increased as time went by. Often on summer evenings
they must have walked the quiet river bank and caught
their reflections in the water where Robert had cleared
a space in the reeds. Or they would climb the hill out
of the village to the open heath and walk among the
prickly furze to make a posy for her dress from the
harebells and the ling.

What were they like, these two lovers who lived before the marvels of photography could capture their
likeness for others to see? No one can tell. But it is certain that they were so closely and admirably suited to
one another that the village folk could hardly wait for
their coming together in church. A rare wedding that
would be and one to be long remembered. No doubt
that during the summer of 1822 the couple were plan-
ning the details of their future life together as they re-
sted in the evenings, for she was not as strong as she
would have liked to be. There were days when she was
not well enough to come out at all and she would send

word to Robert by a farm boy. Such times the hours went by with miserable slowness for both of them.

When autumn came and cooler winds stirred the rushes along the river's edge, Mary's cough became too severe for them to meet there. Robert watched her anxiously, seeing the loved face become thin and pale from her illness. As she declined, so he became ever more loving and attentive. Soon he gave up his work and his separate interests entirely in order to spend every possible moment at her side.

Mary was now confined to her bed, uncomplaining of pain but beset by a strange fear. It was something that had seized her mind with horror ever since the possibility had first occurred to her. Yet she could not bring herself to talk of it. The fear hung like a shadow between the lovers until his endless concern and desire to share every secret with her, persuaded Mary to confess. It was not, she said, a fear of dying. After all, if that should happen it was the Lord's doing and something that must be endured by all. But there had been talk in the village of grave robbers, cruel and heartless people who desecrated the burial places to secure the bodies. Resurrectionists, some people called them. It often happened, particularly when a young body was newly buried, that such ghouls would disinter the corpse in order to sell it to the medical schools for dissection. Her deep and ever present fear was of such a thing happening to her.

Robert calmed and soothed her, begging her not to think of such things. To try to make her forget he bent all his efforts on doing things that he thought would please her. And to please him, she would smile gratefully as if all was well. But as her illness progressed, her fears increased. It was little enough, amid all the feelings of despair that engulfed Robert, to promise anything that would ease her mind. Yes, if she should die he would keep watch over her grave. No stranger would be able to approach that hallowed spot – no one would come to disturb her sleep. The promise seemed to do much to set Mary's mind at rest.

She died as winter set in with its mournful sighing about the river banks and its desolate grip on the once warm heath. On the day of the funeral the bitter winds carried into the church the pain and disappointment of all the village that this was not the service of joyful union that they had looked forward to. When the funeral was over, Robert remained by the grave that held all that had any meaning in his life. He stayed there alone until the next morning when daylight and a waking village precluded the activities of any grave robbers. Then he went home to rest through the few hours of the short winter day before returning to his vigil at the grave-side. For long week after week he followed the routine with steadfast determination, considering health and life itself of little importance beside the need to keep his promise. He became gaunt and ragged and somehow removed from everyday village life so that those few people who saw him shook their heads sadly and made no effort to communicate with him. However, a kindly and sympathetic woman whose cottage lay close to the churchyard gave him lodgings there so that he would never be far removed from Mary's grave.

Robert watched over the mound throughout the long winter. In the rain and frost the earth had sunk a little and sometimes had been all but lost under a heavy fall of snow but by early spring new grass was beginning to grow over the clay. Robert gradually recognised that the vigil had accomplished its purpose. There was no longer any fear that the resurrectionists would disturb that grave. Yet he relinquished his watch without satisfaction or relief, knowing that coming to terms with the everyday world again would be hard to accomplish. Ending the vigil was the final farewell. There was nothing else that he wanted of life.

During May, assisted by the concern and attention of his landlady, Robert gradually regained something of his health, though his spirit seemed never to recover. When the flowers came out along the river bank and the kingfisher darted along the stretch of water he knew so well, he could not bring himself to walk there any more. One bright June morning he went up to his room in the cottage and brought down the few worldly goods he possessed to give to his landlady. Like a ghost already he went to the river and untied the small boat he had once used for fishing. He pulled out from the reeds into the centre channel and disappeared from sight.

Early next day the boat was found capsized in that calm and placid stream. Robert was never seen alive again.

The Graves of Sibton Green

And what did you see out there on the common, Samuel, that faraway night of the double deaths? And what was it drove you mad with its grisly shape and its voices, after the bodies were put to rest in a common grave on the corner of the Green?

Whatever it was it is all forgotten now. The village folk of Sibton sleep well o' nights, if the peaceful look of the place is any guide. The whispers that once told of a violence so intense that it continued from the throes of death into the realm of spirits agonised with their memories, are now silent. No one feels any reluctance to tread that rural path where the simpleton Samuel came gibbering and running from the horror he had seen nor does anyone remember the aftermath of the crime when fear and superstition confused the facts with hearsay and tittle-tattle and clouded the summer days with nameless dread. There were tales of spectral voices, of bodies luminous in the dark, of faces evil beyond imagining. It was enough to frighten a simple person out of his wits.

Nowadays we are well-equipped, what with our enlightened scepticism and our scientific certainties, to withstand the forces that once deeply influenced village life-forces of darkness and ignorance in which demons and phantoms roamed too close to cottage doors. Modern materialism has its faults but at least it has helped to crowd out and disperse the fogs of unwarrantable superstition and unprofitable fears. How much is true, how much is legend in the tales that earlier generations have handed down is something for the individual to decide. Here in Sibton there was a great deal of the latter but there was also much that was clear and factual, including the bare practicality of returning to the cold earth the two dark bodies fallen from their wounds at the Green's edge.

Perhaps a good deal could have been told by Samuel, had he the ability and the will to talk. But he was one of a simple nature of a kind found regularly in villages at one time whose widely proclaimed idiocy often lay in nothing more valid than the possession of a hare lip or a roofless mouth. Samuel was one of the latter – destined to a lifetime of rejection and ridicule through his difficulty in enunciation. His words were ever lost in the listener's impatience with someone who was obviously soft in the head.

What was it that Samuel saw that night of brutal double murder and what was it that haunted him in the weeks that followed before his mind could stand the solitary burden no longer and slid into complete insanity?

No one could tell for certain, though there were many now who listened and tried to construe his nonsense into their own vocabulary. All that was known was that on that fateful day, alone and early, he had come upon the bodies lying unnaturally on the corner of the Green. A closer inspection showed the sudden horror of blood and of flesh gashed and beaten and Samuel had fled in fright to the village, mouthing and bellowing. There was little sense to be made of it until his urgent gestures, indicating the way he had come, persuaded one or two of the men with more patience or more curiosity than the others, to follow him. Within a hundred yards of the fatal spot the simpleton gibbered wildly, pointed the way but ran off in great agitation towards the wooden hut that was his home.

The bodies lay there in the dew-laden grass a few yards apart with their knives fallen bloodily beside them. They were newly dead, and grotesquely sprawled, both dark of hair and of skin. In the gathering crowd of gawping villagers no one could think of aught beyond the dumb spectacle save that these were not local folk that they knew but gippos from the camp outside the village. Gippos or not, the sight was such that two of the women fainted on the spot and for long after the mere recollection of the scene brought nightmares to many who were there.

It was a cruelty and hate beyond thinking, expressed in the utter finality of that fight to the death from a motive no one could even guess. To people inured to the experience of suffering and death among four-footed creatures the sight was no less devastating. Rabbits could scream in their traps in the dawn hours with no one to heed them overmuch but humans were expected to die in their beds with a proper decorum and respect. Even gippos. For a few hours the awesome fact of the deed itself was enough for local stomachs but very soon the underlying mystery of the affair aroused the villagers' speculations. Who were the two men committed to this hideous affray in the hey-day of their lives and what was it in their histories that fed such a desire for mutual destruction?

The answers lay among the gipsy caravans, closed and shuttered suddenly against curious eyes and awkward questions and it was a period of some weeks before a kind of story emerged. How much of this was imagined, how much assisted by gossip and prejudice it is impossible to say but the crux of the matter apparently lay in family jealousy, long festering in the gipsy camp. The two dead men were brothers, it seemed, sons of the headman of that branch of the tribe and one of them illegitimate. Because their father had rejected his first wife, their rightful son had been banished with her to a separate caravan on the edge of the encampment. In his stead the illegitimate son was favoured and made much of by the headman and his new wife. Jealousy and the need for revenge lay deep in the situation. In the way of life that they knew, the brothers saw physical combat to the death as the only solution.

In the end it came to the brutal fact of mutual murder on the quiet edge of Sibton Green. No one – except perhaps poor Samuel – saw that terrible fight but the multiplicity of blows and slashes on the bodies suggested that they fought with a bestial desperation long after ordinary mortals would have yielded to death.

It is not surprising that the emotions that were too intense to be contained in their living bodies should remain after all else was gone and the neighbourhood of the deed became a place whose atmosphere was charged with supernatural agonies. The villagers soon came to speak of it in terms of dread. Poor Samuel, who was not seen for weeks after his frightening experience, could not be dragged by the officials of the law to visit the spot again and in his fears and anxieties gradually lost what articulation he had possessed and with it his reason. When the gipsies were buried, close by where the fatal conflict took place, many a wise woman presaged evil to come.

Were there faces in the trees there in the wood beside the Green – faces luminous and ghostly as many claimed? Were there hideous spectres, malformed beyond belief, beneath leaves that dripped with blood? Many held such things to be true, often people who most assuredly had never been near, but that the area was haunted came to be known and accepted, even by those who had doubts, by the experiences of credible witnesses. Prominent among them was the schoolmaster, whose devotion to truth no one could question.

A naturalist and keen observer of every form of wild life, the schoolmaster chose Saturday mornings for his favourite jaunts well away from the school and into the woods that in those days bordered the Green. As the foremost of the sceptics on the subject of supernatural forces in the village, it no doubt gave him considerable pleasure to feel that his superior scientific beliefs freed him from the fears of simpler folk and allowed him to delve with proper objectivity into the world of natural history.

It was with a distinct lack of objectivity that he came hurtling out of the wood on the second Saturday after the killings, with his clothes in disarray, his wig awry, his face covered in sweat from so much haste. Just as the locals were tasting their first draught of the day the distraught schoolmaster arrived before them, thankful for the sanity of recognisable old men innocently refreshing themselves. Shakily, he accepted a tankard of ale and thanked God for his deliverance. As for his experiences in the wood he spoke not a word and none among those present questioned him or cared to smile.

The old men looked towards the Green and the wood and then at the schoolmaster and then at each other. One of them raised his tankard and nodded sagely into the bottom of it.

"Better to leave them things be," he mumbled. They all nodded. Ah, they thought, it was better to leave them things be.

The Fantastical Little Ghost

The story of the 'fantastical' little Ghost of Dagworth Hall came to me in a roundabout sort of way through a fortuitous happening of over a hundred years ago when a certain local historian and general busybody in that corner of Suffolk became interested in the supernatural.

In the course of his enquiries he one day accosted a horseman on a large farm nearby. The horseman was busy unloading sacks of meal from a waggon and expressed some impatience with such questions.

"Ghosts? Do I look as if I believe in ghosts?" he demanded, pulling another sack to the edge of the waggon. "I've got better things to think of. Catch me wasting time on such nonsense – I've forgot all the tales I've heard about such things."

He humped the last sack on to his shoulder and took it away into the corn shed. After a minute he came back dusting his clothes smartly with his hands. With the job finished it seemed he could look a little more indulgently at the question. "No, never seen a ghost and I don't suppose I ever shall. I seen plenty o' corn sacks – I can tell you that. I seen plenty o' hard work!"

"Sorry to have troubled you," the interrogator apologised.

"That don't mean to say," the horseman went on rather crossly as if he had been deliberately asked the wrong questions, "that don't mean to say I ain't seen

91

the weppers."

"Weppers?"

"That's right. People call 'em weppers. We hereabouts, we always call 'em the lantern-men. You can come across the lantern-men now and agin – they're like little lights moving about."

"Oh, you mean vapours!"

"That's right. I seen 'em many a time when I've bin working – seen 'em all over the place. Course, in my job, I been out in all weathers, day an' night. I seen 'em scores o' times, running around. They fare to come out o' the ground and run all over the place. Yes, that was the lantern-men sure enough."

The questioner resigned himself to hearing about the lantern-men though it was by no means the sort of phenomenon he was interested in. The horseman, however, his thoughts kindled into a blaze of recollections, went on in some detail.

"Folks do say," he assured the listener, "that if one man stand at one end of a field and another stand opposite him in the other corner and they whistle to one another, the lantern-men will always run to the whistle. It's a good thing to know this when you're working in the fields because the lantern-man will always try to come up against you and to kill you if so be he is able."

Since the visitor showed less interest and belief than expected in "weppers" the horseman soon returned to his original mood of morose resentment. "Ghosts," he repeated with as much contempt as he could get into the word. "You want to hear about a ghost – you go and see old Betsy Moore at her cottage." He shifted himself as if he felt that he had already spent too much time on such things but called out just before he disappeared into the barn: "Course, that's only a little owd ghost."

Later that same day the enquirer made his way to Betsy Moore's cottage and was soon sitting beside the fire with the old woman sitting opposite and wrinkling up her face with the efforts of recollection.

"That happened years and years ago up at Dagworth Hall – you don't know it, you say? Not know Dagworth Hall? Everybody know it," she said severely. "That was when Sir Osborn – Sir Osborn something-or-other lived there long afore my time."

Her thoughts would wander off to other things and he found that every now and then he must prompt her to bring her back to the subject of the little ghost.

"Yes," she said once, "it was little ghost – a fantastical little ghost but I don't know so much about it being a story. I always took it to be the truth, something that happened just the same as anything else. I was only a child when I was told about it but that's stayed in my mind ever since. I ain't ever told anyone afore."

The old lady sank into a silence then and the visitor prompted her again as he was required to do from time to time during her rambling story. Without the long lapses, the frequent inconsequential mutterings, the essential story that the visitor set down was this:

At the time when Sir Osborn was at the Hall it was a house full of life and gaiety. There were 'high jinks' as old Betsy put it, in which the five children of the family were generally involved. Sir Osborn's beautiful wife was a lady of indulgent tendencies who allowed the children to spread themselves so audibly and effectively through the Hall that one would have thought there were twenty of them.

In fact, even to the children themselves there often

seemed to be more than the true number of them. In their midst of a game there would be something – something extra to their own playing, something a little different from their own voices yet mingling so closely in the confusion that it was long before they could believe that it was not one of themselves. "Play again, play again," a voice would cry, shrill with excitement. Was it one of themselves who said it? Who had such a wee small voice?

The children played their boisterous games in the hall, in the bedrooms and corridors, in the garden and sometimes even in the copse beyond the garden. Wherever they were, the puzzlement stayed with them. There was someone else or something else that interpolated itself into their excitements. One day there happened to be a momentary hush as the children considered what game to play next and in the quiet came the unmistakeable small voice of a strange child. "Play again, play again," it said but the children could see nothing nor understand where the voice came from and they fled in utter fright to the kitchen.

Yet, as time went on and seeing no harm in the childish spirit, the children became used to the sixth presence in their game and gradually the whole household swallowed their superstitious fears and accepted the little one. The prevailing mood now became one of curiosity. If the spirit could say "Play again", and "Play with me" in its thin little voice, surely it must be able to say other things. Unwillingly at first, as it seemed, the little one was slowly persuaded to talk about himself. Most of what he said was of childish things, of games and of mischiefs and sometimes he complained of being hungry. At those times the children would put out food on platters about the house and in very little time it had disappeared.

"Can't we see you?" the family wanted to know, for the wraith soon became very real to them and though apparently absent from the house for most of the day, it engaged more and more in converse with the humans. No, the small voice said, only once could he be seen, only once and when the right time came he would show himself. His voice was sometimes lively, sometimes sad. If the children were not playing he would play alone, hiding objects, rolling or catching them or singing as he sat on the rocking horse.

His name was Malkin, he once told the children and he really belonged to another house nearby. That was where his mother and brothers lived and they were usually rather cross with him for leaving them to go and converse with living people. But it seemed that Sir Osborn's lively family had captivated the little ghost. It spent more and more time in the house, unseen but obviously present and always went back unwillingly to its proper house and family. One in particular among the children seemed to fascinate the wayward Malkin. It was Emilia, the older blonde daughter, and she was equally attached to him. Much of what was ever learned about Malkin came through the girl's affectionate concern and as he spoke she listened with increasing curiosity.

He was born at Lavenham, Malkin confided one day. He had lived as a human for seven years in the midst of a large family. The family was poor, his father was a farm labourer and his mother had to work hard in the home. At harvest time that year when he was seven years old she went into the fields each day to glean and she would take one or more of the children with her.

On this certain day Malkin went alone with his mother. He could not keep up with her and she laid him on a little bed of straw to rest in the sun. Probably he had gone to sleep, for he could remember very little else except that he woke up suddenly and there were strange people and they picked him up and took him away.

"Are you happy now?" Emilia asked him. Malkin considered. "I like to play," he said. "I like all the games you play. But I shall not always be as I am. Already I have been in this present condition for seven years and there will be another seven, I believe, before I change. After that, I don't know. Yes, I think I am happy – I am happy enough."

Time after time Emilia begged to be able to see him. In the end, apparently with a good deal of reluctance, he gave in. There were two conditions, he told her. It must be for her eyes alone and also, while he was visible she must on no account touch him. Emilia agreed and eagerly awaited the moment of revelation when she would see her playmate as a physical being.

At the time appointed she was in the nursery alone, save for Malkin who was obviously playing with the abacus in the corner.

"You promised," she reminded him.

He seemed to sigh, like any living child summoned to leave a plaything, though the words he spoke seemed to come from older lips. "You should not have asked," he said sadly. "It won't be at all as you think."

The abacus stopped rattling, small footsteps came across the floor towards her and when they stopped he was suddenly standing there. Emilia stared silently at her little friend. He was, indeed, very small, even younger than she had imagined, dressed in a frayed

96

white frock and unkempt as if he had been lying in some straw. In fact, he was picking small bits of straw from his hair and crying and not looking at Emilia at all. In another moment he seemed to be struggling, fighting against unseen, clutching hands, fighting with puny fists, gasping and sobbing in the knowledge of his weakness.

Shocked, Emilia jumped up and would have gone to aid the little one against whatever it was that assailed him but he screamed: "Don't touch me," and before her eyes he seemed to be lifted and borne off into the darkness.

When she recovered, Emilia tried to find Malkin again. She and the whole family searched the house, calling out for him and putting platters of food wherever he might be hidden. But Emilia wept, bitterly regretting her importunity and realising now that she had asked too much of Malkin and that he had given too much. He would never come back again.

The Witch of
Scrapfaggot Green

"Yew aren't a-goin' to ast me about that owd
ghost, are ye?" he said, leaning on his spade
and preparing himself for the worst.

"I was thinking about it," I said, as I looked admir-
ingly over the gate into the well-kept garden. "As you
live nearby I thought you'd know about it. Did it
trouble you very much?"

"Trouble? No, that owd ghost di'n't cause a lot o'
trouble. Them reporters caused the trouble. One
time, a few year ago, yew cou'n't move in the village for
strangers – all askin' silly questions. I allus reckoned
that if every one on 'em had brought a spade stid of
a camera, they could ha' dug my garden an' done a lot
more good."

"You didn't see any ghost?"

"No, nor yit heard it. Nor I di'n't hear them church
bells that was supposed to ring." His eyes twinkled.
"Haps them there reporters ha' got sharper ears than
I hev. I di'n't hear any church bells nor see no owd
witches on a broomstick. Still, yew hev a yarn with my
neighbour. He may know a lot more'n I dew, him bein'
the village nosey-parker. Dew yew ast him."

I thanked the man with the spade and withdrew,
after a few complimentary words on his garden. However, I was in no hurry to interview the neighbour,
preferring the honest opinion of a non-believer to
someone who might produce any tale to suit his own

importance. The ghost of Scrapfaggot Green in Great Leighs had been the subject of intense attention a few years before, when a variety of hair-raising claims were made on behalf of the ghost in the national press. Coming at a time when other domestic news was scarce and being a genuine post-war phenomenon somehow linked to witchery and U.S. army trucks, there was room for a good deal of conjecture and imagination.

The trouble is that the more a ghost story is embellished, the less credible it becomes. Locals like my gardening friend learned to use a largish pinch of salt with many of the tales sent off to London. Certainly there was a ghost and certainly strange and unaccountable things happened in the pub at the Green there about forty years ago. But was there a mummified cat and a witch's tall hat found later in a bricked-up room? It sounds too perfect to be true. And did the chickens commit suicide in the water-butts as the bells rang at midnight? The gardener who lived by the church knew nothing of it.

Nevertheless, even without the legends that grew up on the fringe of the ghost-hunt, the story is a good one. To start with, there was something that placed this particular visitant far above those others whose fates are bound to conventional settings in old houses and lonely churchyards. For this was the ghost of a witch, a poor creature who had lived in the area long ago and had apparently dealt in all the complicated rigmarole of her craft. Her association with the inn and in particular with the guest bed-room is difficult to understand but it was there that the haunting was concentrated. It began suddenly towards the end of the war as if this volatile spirit had suddenly been released – as indeed it is believed to have been – by some disturb-

100

ing human agency.

The witch's ghost lost no time in making its presence known, being particularly noisy and unsympathetic to any who might believe that a bedroom should be a place of peace and repose. Consternation at its disturbing behaviour led the landlord to lock the bedroom unless its accommodation was urgently needed and the room tended to become a handy storing place for goods not in actual use. A carton of electric light bulbs was placed beside the bed early on in the saga of witchery. Next day, despite the locked door, they were found dispersed to unlikely places all over the room.

It was a procedure that soon became all too familiar. Any objects left in the room were liable to be removed or lost or even smashed. Even more alarming was the noise that accompanied these activities. Furniture was apparently being moved about, though usually found in the same spot next day and there was the sound of boots scuffing the floor. There was a kind of feverish agitation in all the sounds that was frightening to hear. One morning when the haunted room was opened, the wardrobe was found dismantled and lying in its three separate parts. It was an ingenious achievement that was repeated several times during the weeks following.

However, the business of the pub had to go on and now and again a guest was put in the haunted room when no other accommodation was available. For more than one it turned out to be a very long night and a very hair-raising experience. A north-country commercial traveller left at an early hour next morning after enduring what he claimed was a continous racket of furniture moving that deprived him of sleep. Some time later, a young woman required a room. Since all other rooms were occupied, the landlord regretfully handed her the key of the haunted room.

It was a night that she would remember for the rest of her life. Being tired after travelling all day she soon fell asleep but after a short period suddenly awoke, feeling convinced that there was someone else in the room. With senses sharpened by fear, she sat up to peer around her into the shadows. Quite close by the bed, almost looming over her, was a misty, moving shape that menacingly circled the bed. Too overcome with horror even to cry out, the girl watched the shape slowly move away. In a few moments it had disappeared. The girl switched on the light and found the room was empty but she was too upset by the experience to go back to sleep. For the remainder of the night she sat by the window, shivering and waiting in the daylight.

By now there was a good deal of interest in the Scrapfaggot ghost. Why had it suddenly become so active and so malevolent, people wondered? Among the villagers there were some who knew or shrewdly guessed the answer but like country folk everywhere were unwilling to proffer an opinion. It was almost by accident that the truth was discovered, when a reporter stayed to have a cup of tea at one of the cottages. The two elderly sisters living there were delighted to have a chat with someone from faraway London and it was only once or twice when a noisy U.S. army truck went by, that the conversation was interrupted.

"I've got nothing against those boys," one of the ladies said, going to close the window, "but they do stir up the dust."

"Not the only thing they stir up," her sister retorted unexpectedly and the reporter noted the quick look and the silence that followed. It took some skilful interrogation and several cups of tea before the sisters felt obliged to divulge what they thought was the cause of the haunting. It all began when the U.S. forces had first come to use the airfield nearby and found this secondary approach past the cottages to be too narrow for their massive vehicles. The lane was widened all the way along and among other material summarily thrown aside was a huge boulder that had lain about half a mile from the sisters' cottage. In this part of the country such a boulder was a rare thing indeed but it occasioned no more than a passing interest in the road workers.

To the sisters it was a calamity for that boulder had secured the witch's grave. That spot was where she had been buried and the stone was placed to prevent her doing further mischief. By this extraordinary confluence of ancient and modern circumstances, the witch's ghost was released. There would be more trouble, the old ladies thought, because she had been a most powerful witch.

There was more trouble. The most spectacular trouble came one morning after a calm and quiet night in July. Cottagers came out to find what might have been expected after a hurricane. Fences were down, implements damaged, straw and hay spread everywhere, hand tools blown or thrown into the fields. It seemed certain that it must be the work of a demented spirit, the frantic witch of Scrapfaggot. It was time, the villagers decided, for measures to be taken.

The measures, by general, unspoken agreement, entailed returning the boulder to its original position over the witch's grave. But would this be enough? Should there be spells and incantations spoken suitable to a witch's burial place? No, the villagers decided, they would not be a party to such outlandish goings-on. Just put the stone back and hope for the best. At least it could not make matters worse.

The experiment proved to be a stunning success. At the moment that the boulder was rolled back into its long-accustomed place the haunting ceased. Army trucks rumbled around the grave without any great inconvenience. The reporters went home and the public spotlight on this remote corner quickly diminished. The ghost of the witch of Scrapfaggot Green would trouble no one ever again – while the boulder remained over her grave.

However, the story was not quite played out, though it was a few years later when this bizarre footnote was added. It concerns a group of three old-style cottages in Great Leigh that were bought with the idea of turning them into one dwelling. Building alterations went on without interruption in two of the cottages but the third, though identical, presented a series of unexpected hold-ups and difficulties partly because its whole atmosphere was so foetid and repellent. The upper floor especially was charged with a sense of hideous, long-kept secrets. A dog that was encouraged to mount the stairs fled howling out of the building and showed signs of complete terror. Without doubt this had been the house of the witch.

With considerable misgivings, the workmen began on the upper floor and immediately discovered a small, secret room that had been completely bricked up. If this had once been the inner sanctum of the witch's activities, what horrors might it still hold? Could there be powers of evil left hidden in the room that were likely to be released? These thoughts must have been in the minds of the renovators who were nevertheless committed to the task of dismantling the secret room. When the wall was knocked down the tiny room was still dark. There was a smell of dust and damp rubble that did not obliterate that other smell – of potions and concoctions and private experiments of long ago. Hesitantly, the cell was illuminated. There were only two recognisable objects. In a corner stood a tall witch's hat and beside it the black mummified corpse of a cat.

The Hound of the Storm

Bachelor Jonathon Prowling, being long of leg and untrammeled by companions, overtook his neighbours Walt and Jessie Bedingrass with their two children on the way to church that Sunday morning in early August. Jonathon would have been content with raising his hat and striding on but Walt called out: "Hold you hard, Jonathon. Bells ain't started tolling yet. I reckon parson will keep us there long enough without our help."

Not unwilling, Jonathon fell in step with the Bedingrass family, half envying the staid Walt his comely wife and spirited children. "That's just habit," he said, "walking quick – not because I want to get ahead of other folk."

He met the smiles of the two children, a boy of ten and a girl a year or so younger and noted that, despite the sunny morning, they were equipped to withstand a downpour of rain. Walt caught his look of surprise and said: "Jessie reckon there'll be a storm. Trouble is she's nearly always right. She seem to sense a storm coming afore there's a sign of it in the sky. I long ago gave up arguing about it. That'll rain sure enough if Jessie say so."

"Well, the sky do begin to look a bit funny ahead there. But the sun is still shining – d'you know I was out in the fields at seven this morning just in my shirt and breeches and the air was as warm and pure as midday. A few more days and I shall be sharpening my old scythe again for the harvest."

But Jessie Bedingrass was shaking her head. "That ain't to my liking," she said, "this day, that don't come properly natural to my way of thinking."

She hustled the children along, cluttered though they were and hot with the sun on their backs. In a few minutes the small party entered the porch of the parish church in Bungay and joined the considerable congregation there. Walt had been right enough – there was still time to say a prayer and to gaze around with awe at the fine interior. In the pews round about were many familiar faces and figures that somehow endowed the solemnity of the occasion with a glow of friendliness.

Almost as soon as they had opened their prayer books, the congregation noted the dwindling light. The sun that had ushered them along country roads to the church now disappeared and a dark and threatening gloom took its place with an unnatural speed. In Jessie Bedingrass's glance at her husband above the childrens' heads there was due satisfaction at having been right again but concern too for the family in the storm that was sure to be.

The rain came suddenly, beating like an army's complement of kettle-drums on the windows and roof. Voices went on singing and intoning but the sound was soon completely lost in the vicious lashing without. Lips moved without meaning and eyes were turned upwards towards the windows as if fearful that they would crack or give way before such unwonted hammering. The Rector stood upon the step before the lectern, silent and impotent, waiting for the noise to subside. Then, as it continued unabated, he raised his hands and gestured that the people should be seated.

Suddenly, over the roar and wash of the rain came the first ear-splitting crack of thunder, following so close behind a flash of lightning that it seemed almost at one. Despite their mother's arm about them as they huddled in the pew, the Bedingrass children were crying in sheer disbelief at the enormity of the noise and when the second blinding flash of lightning heralded the thunder and lit up the whole of the interior for one frightening, garish moment, it seemed to them that the very walls were shaking. The whole congregation stood aghast at the violence of the thunder and the service was forgotten. They huddled together in family groups as lightning preceded thunder in a continuous barrage and still accompanied by the frenzied beating of the rain. Some would have fled, so frightened were they of imminent disaster and sudden death and convinced that this was some direct visitation upon the church but the storm outside was of such proportions that no one dared to offer himself to such power.

Those who were devout fell on their knees and prayed. Jonathon Prowling, close by the Bedingrass family, looked up to the roof and felt the whole edifice shake above him. In the deafening noise he too, prayed, not for deliverance but for the reason of all dumb animals that would be driven to terror by the storm. There were several of the congregation about him who were inaudibly crying and shouting in their panic, holding hands to their ears after each lightning flash in order to withstand the vehemence of the thunder. Others were bemused, as if the storm had taken their senses but all were gripped by a deadly fear of some doom that seemed about to fall.

It came suddenly at the height of the noise and con-

109

fusion when the great outer doors of the church crashed open. Immediately in the doorway appeared a form of something distorted and beast-like on four legs and black as the blackest night, as like a great, pestilential dog as anything, if name could be found for such horror. In the flashes of lightning the black beast could be seen coming into the body of the church and now the people who had been frightened before were ready to give up their wits and their hope, believing that their last hour had come. For at least two of those present, the fear was to come true.

The black beast – or dog as some held it to be when comparing their experiences later – looked neither to right nor left but ran swiftly down the central aisle at what seemed the speed of the devil himself. Then fitfully, as the flashes lit the church, it could be seen moving about amongst the congregation and the terror of the intermittent darkness became even greater than that of the creature's horrid, visible aspect. Without pause it glided from pew to pew. In one place, where two worshippers on their knees barred its way, it passed them with a hideous ferocity, in one instant throwing them back with their necks broken, dying even as they prayed. Others who felt the fiend brushing past them were burned where they were touched and would carry the scars evermore to remind them of this ill-begotten day.

Of those few who still believed that this was no visitation of the devil but some wild beast somehow created in the storm, was Jonathon Prowling. As fearful as any of the power of the monstrous dog, he had seen the sudden death of two of his friends and yet felt it within him to try to protect the Bedingrass children as it came near. All around, people were suddenly scattering as

110

they caught sight of the beast or giving way to fainting fits when there seemed to be no way of escape. The Bedingrass children screamed as the monster showed itself nearby and Jonathon stood and shielded them, hoping that it would rush past in pursuing its mad course. Instead, the movement that Jonathon made seemed to enrage the animal. It stopped, fixed red eyes on him for a moment then leapt upon him, gripped him with its slavering jaws in the back as he turned and then savagely took its way to the door and disappeared.

Jonathon lay on the floor as if dead. His body was strangely shrunken and drawn together, it was said, like a leather purse pulled tight with its string. Others believed he had the appearance of one scorched and dehydrated by fire. But, dead or not, the remaining parishioners had no wish to stay a moment longer. As the storm abated and the vicious lightning flashes seemed to follow the dog elsewhere, they fled without dignity to their homes, only thankful that their own lives had been spared.

Though it seemed incredible to those who had witnessed the attack, Jonathon survived. Over a long period he recovered to an extent that he could follow the routine of everyday life again but it was seen that he was a changed man. His neighbours the Bedingrassess reported that he acted very strangely sometimes and the children insisted that they had heard him barking like a dog. He lived for many years as proof of the experiences on that August Sunday morning in 1577 when he and staid country folk came to a painfully close confrontation with the devil. If more proof were needed, sceptics would be taken to the doorway of the church where the beast's claws had gouged the timber and where even the stonework bore record of the furious talons.

The storm had come with a supernatural intensity that day and subsided at Bungay with the same abruptness. But it was not the end of the visitation. On the same day and accompanied by the same frightening noise of a violent storm, the black beast appeared at Blythburgh. As at Bungay, it entered the church there and in sight of the terror-stricken congregation sat himself upon a beam that had once supported the rood. It stayed there for a minute while the storm raged outside and then grasped a rope that hung from the roof and swung itself right through the church over the peoples' heads. Twice it swung, black and menacing overhead like the devil himself. Then suddenly the beast dropped, landed on the innocent figures of two men and a boy who were come here to join in the quiet rituals of a prayer service but who were now slain instantly, all three without a single moan. And their neighbour in the pew, his life spared, suffered hideous burns and scars for his lifetime through his momentary contact with the beast.

Long ago it happened, in those two separate churches on a summer's day when the corn was coming up ripe for harvest. In sober retrospect those who were present and witnessed the visitation set down the facts without disagreement, telling only that which they knew to be true so that later generations of sceptics, such as you and I, will perforce believe that such a thing undoubtedly took place.

Moving House

I came to East Anglia for the first time about ten years ago. Before then I had lived in the West Country and I was prepared for some contrasts when I was unexpectedly sent to work in this area. Of course, I knew from reputation some of the main features of Norfolk and Suffolk but I found many surprises, nevertheless, not just in the geography but in people, their habits and speech, all different though I could not always say what the difference was. The one thing I had been certain about was that East Anglia was flat. Everybody said so. East Anglia? Flat, they said, as if that disposed of the whole area. I found, in fact, that flatness was a minor ingredient in a landscape of infinite variety and now join with local people in swearing that East Anglia is not flat – only a bit flatter than some other parts.

I may seem to go on a bit about this but because of the kind of work I was doing in calling on farmers, the topography was a fairly important ingredient of my daily grind. Large-scale maps were endlessly consulted but often lacked the local information that would be useful to a rather stupid stranger having to find small hamlets and distant farms. Some of the farms were so remote I wondered sometimes how people ever reached them. They would be miles away from the village in which they were supposed to be situated and seldom signposted so that I would arrive at a farm after an exhausting drive only to be told that it wasn't Ash Farm but Oak Farm. Ash Farm was on the other side of the village.

I discovered that a complex arrangement of minor roads and farm tracks would baulk my intentions time after time. A promising-looking lane that seemed to go in the right direction would come to an abrupt end while some meandering track that seemed too humble for anything but a goat-cart would suddenly open up to reveal a very modern type of farm. There was a doubtful value in asking a passer-by for directions, even if you are lucky enough to find anyone to ask, since he would know the area by local names that had no answer on my map. Often there was little help to be distilled from the advice so cheerfully and unwillingly given until the local raised his hand and pointed. Being pointed in the right direction became the basis of my searching on many a day.

There was one particular morning in early summer when I set out to find Willow Farm. I could easily find the village on the map but the farm itself could be anywhere within several square miles. All I knew, from an earlier phone call, was that it had a large and distinctive Dutch barn. I therefore drove to a convenient high point which gave a view over several fields and was relieved to see the very farm about a mile away. Knowing that I was following the right general direction, I drove along narrow and winding roads of the sort I was becoming very familiar with, when a broad verge at the side invited me to pull up and look at the map again.

It was a lovely morning. The sun was pouring over the hedge beside me right on to a farmhouse on the other side of the road. I had not noticed it when I

114

pulled up. I was so surprised I got out of the car and walked across. It was the most beautiful farmhouse I had ever seen, with a cluster of drowsy-looking buildings huddling close like something once seen in a fairytale. The house was basking in the sunlight, with the honey-coloured thatched roof over-hanging timbered walls and leaded-glass windows that reflected the colours of the luxuriant garden. There were pergolas and a summer-house and everywhere a kind of joyful and irresistable bounty of growth that veiled the earth intirely. There seemed to be no one about but work had been done recently for there were old-fashioned round corn-stacks in the yard, so small and neat they could have been built by gnomes and fairies.

I must come and have another look, I promised myself, remembering that it was getting late for my appointment at Willow Farm. Later that day I did come back – at least I thought I did but I must have taken a wrong turning because I couldn't see the farm that had so fascinated me. It was vexing but considering the maze of by-ways in that area not at all surprising. I would come and find it on my day off.

When that day came I started from the same hill and went in the same general direction as before. I did not pass the farm. I tried parallel roads and farm tracks and sometimes felt certain I was in the right place but could not have been because there was no farm. Questions in the village yielded nothing chiefly because I knew of no names to ask for and similar enquiries among my colleagues only produced a mixed collection of jokes about mirages and such fancies.

It was during August and just before the harvest began that I had another puzzling experience in connection with the elusive farm. I had been going over

115

the location again and was convinced that I had got to the very spot where I had originally pulled up. I stopped on what seemed to be the same piece of open verge but all I saw was a farm-worker walking towards me from far up the road. At least, I thought, he will know all about this immediate locality and will be just the person to ask.

I suppose I busied myself with maps and things for a few minutes as the man, wearing some kind of old-fashioned smock, came towards me very slowly. When I looked up, assuming that he must now be almost abreast of my car, he was not there. He must have gone into the fields at the side, I guessed and went to the hedge to look over. There was nothing but a great field of wheat on that side so I crossed the road to the spot where I thought I had seen the farmhouse. All that was there was a small field or paddock looking very neglected and overgrown with clumps of brambles and thistles encroaching in the rough grass. There was a short and crumbling fence around most of the area with a straggling apple tree in the corner and an old horse-drawn drill almost rotten with age half hidden in the nettles. Unexpectedly, among some piles of mossy bricks, was a rambler rose, supine and half-strangled but still alive.

Well, the man must have got through a gap and crossed the paddock for he was certainly out of sight now. It was all very frustrating and I could not help feeling irritated with myself for wasting so much time on the unprofitable quest. No more, I told myself, from now on I'll keep to everyday farms with mud in the yard and clanking pails outside the back door.

Next day I was visiting one such farm in the area, occupied by a friendly West Countryman whose accent carried me back to my own earlier days in Somerset. He was in his office and shuffling through some papers in trying to find something while I looked around the room. He was, he had admitted, an amateur artist and one or two of his landscapes were on the wall. One was a painting of a farmhouse, a beautiful compact house of honey-coloured thatch and diamond-leaded windows that reflected the garden flowers –

"That's it!" I almost shouted in excitement. "That's the house I've been looking for. Thank heaven I've found it at last."

He came across and took the picture off the wall, slowly examining it.

"Is this the farm you've been looking for?" he asked.

"That's it! I thought I was never going to find it. Now tell me just where it is."

He smiled and asked me to look at the picture again. "Are you sure? Is this really a good picture of the place you saw?"

"Yes, it's perfect. Even those little round corn stacks and the summer house. How clever of you to paint it. You must have seen it at the same time of the year. All the flowers are just the same."

"The flowers are always the same at that house. As a matter of fact I have never seen it, or the flowers or the rest of it."

"A photograph?"

"Oh, there are no photographs of that house, I am afraid."

"It sounds very mysterious. Surely a house is a house. I've seen it, remember."

"You were lucky. Yes, it is even more mysterious than you think, because my picture is painted from descriptions – all very similar descriptions that agree in

117

every detail that have been given to me. And the people who described it saw this house in Somerset. I painted that picture before I came to East Anglia."

I must have looked my astonishment for he went on: "It is even stranger still, because after painting that picture I have been told that the farmhouse has been seen in Wales, in Shropshire, in Sussex. For all I know, many other places.

"But I saw it," I insisted stubbornly. "It was no more than two miles from here. Couldn't we go and have a look together?"

"No, I am afraid not. This house doesn't exist in bricks and mortar, not now, anyway. Perhaps it did once. But even if you look you won't find it. No one has ever found it twice. But at least console yourself that you have seen it. I haven't and never will because I'm just a bumbling farmer with no sensitivity."

"You think it was just a dream?"

"No, no dream. Too many people have seen the same house in too many different places. But how to explain it I don't know. Best to accept it and forget it. You've had your glimpse and that's it."

I remembered that over-grown paddock and the old man in a smock who had seemed to disappear. "I don't know," I said. "I may just get another half-glimpse. At least I know where to look."

In the bright sunlight of another morning I went to the empty field again and tried to imagine the farmhouse there in all its beauty before the desolation. The rambler rose – was that all that was left? It seemed so. The earth concealed all save for a broken piece of leaded glass and a dais that could have held a summerhouse. And in the farthest corner, an old man in an out-dated smock, who just stood and watched.

Hair Sets and Set-Backs

On the very first day that young Hazel Warren went to work in the hairdressing department of the local Co-op in a village near Colchester, she was told that the place was haunted. Among all the other information and instruction she was given as a novice hand and general assistant, this must have seemed the least importance piece of knowledge of the day. Haunted or not, Hazel was intent on becoming a success in the salon and had no grumbles at having to work very hard at the trivial tasks laid on her by the existing hierarchy of beauticians. Four girls, glamorous and sophisticated looking to Hazel's apprentice eyes, ministered to the clients' needs in the salon, led by Phyllis who had very strict ideas about behaviour and orderliness, everything having to be in its proper place and ready for use. She was obsessive about such things, the younger girls complained, though when eventually Hazel herself became the manageress of the salon she was able to appreciate the good training she had been given.

In her first few weeks, Hazel had to learn a great deal, not only about her Cinderella-like duties but also about her colleagues and about the unexpected difficulty in always having a required object immediately to hand. With the most zealous application to her new job, Hazel could not always produce the sprays and combs, the grips and hairnets, the clips and shampoos

119

from where they were supposed to be because quite frequently they seemed to have been moved. There was a good deal of teasing about this by the other girls but only Phyllis complained openly about what she considered to be slackness in providing whatever she needed at a moment's notice.

"Don't worry," the younger girls said, "it's probably the ghost. Things are always disappearing in this place."

It was certainly a puzzle to Hazel. So often she made a point of putting all the items in their proper places at night only to find that they were somewhere else in the morning. Of course, she could not proclaim this too loudly because Phyllis always arrived first in the morning and could have been responsible. Phyllis would hear no talk of ghosts and Hazel's surprise at finding something in a different place was usually ascribed to her forgetfulness or carelessness.

As the years went by Hazel gradually moved up through the salon hierarchy, becoming a skilled and dedicated hair-dresser well-liked by her colleagues and always sought after by the customers. By now she had become accustomed to the mischievous agency that so regularly moved things in the salon and was inclined to take it in the good humour in which the hide-and-seek seemed to be activated. Some time after she had reached the top post as manageress of the salon considerable structural alterations were made to the store complex in which the hairdressing department was housed. Some new departments were added and a completely different access provided for the hair-dressing salon. In future it would be reached through a glass door at the back of the main shop, the glass door opening directly on to the brand new staircase. The change-over also affected staffing arrangements and it happened that when the salon was re-opened two or three lively new girls came too. The story of the ghost was just the thing to set them giggling and joking and it wasn't long before one of them suggested a seance to try and contact the spirit and ask why it was always moving things around.

The idea seemed rather bizarre to Hazel and she took no part in the proceedings. However, she had no objection to the girls amusing themselves provided it did not interfere with the running of the salon. A Friday evening seemed a good time since, although they were open until eight o'clock, there were seldom any appointments after seven. The seance took place, therefore, one quiet Friday evening at about seven thirty. How it was conducted Hazel could not tell as she was busy bringing the day's routine to an end but it was obviously an occasion for a good deal of fun and laughter. At one point two of the new girls went into a cupboard, dressed a broom in an old-fashioned cape with a wig on top and pretended it was a ghost. They called it Annie, they said because it did not live there any more. Hazel thereupon decided that things had gone far enough and bundled the girls off home just before eight o'clock. Then she made sure that everything in and near the salon was tidy and in its proper place. When she was satisfied that this was so, she locked up and went home.

Next morning she unlocked the main doors at eight o'clock, and walked through the china and glass department to the glass door at the back to reach the stairs. Here she received the first indication that something was wrong. There was a hair spray on the bottom step, lying as if it had been thrown. A little further up was a collection of hair-nets, then more sprays and cosmetics and combs in profusion.

On the landing at the top of the stairs a wire stand which had held hair sprays had been thrown across to the other side and the floor was littered with the containers. A tall wooden cabinet in which a variety of requisites were kept was in place but with the door wide open and the whole paraphernalia of soaps, grips, towels, shampoos and everything else thrown out and strewn over the floor.

Hazel scarcely dared to look into the salon itself. When she did open the door she stood and stared. What had been tidy and immaculate only hours before was now a place of disharmony and confusion. Towels, gowns, overalls which had been so carefully left on pegs and rails were moved to the most unlikely situations on handles, over mirrors, or hanging over chairbacks in some kind of mad or childish design. A chaos of minor requisites from combs to shampoo sachets littered the washstands and, most surprising of all, the heavy foot-rests had been moved. One of these had somehow travelled across the surface of the display table in the centre of the room for it had gouged lines in the wood. Two of the footrests were lying in the sinks and Hazel marvelled that they had not damaged the porcelain.

Yet, apart from the grazed surface of the centre table, there was no great harm done, nothing broken and nothing missing. There was no question of it being a break-in. It was no less frightening, though, to realise that the arrangement of the objects was calculated and that the disarray spoke of anger and indignation rather than of thoughtless destruction. Wisely, Hazel left the scene to speak for itself when the girls arrived

122

for work for there was no doubt in her mind that the demonstration was associated with the hilarious seance of the night before.

It was a sober, thoughtful group of young hairdressers who tended to their clients' needs that day. Violence had come too close, a deliberate measure of violence that carried an implied threat that it could be extended and repeated at any time. They wondered how they could have stirred up such anger and what they could do to placate the power responsible. With many misgivings, the girls decided that they must hold another and more serious seance and try to apologise to the outraged spirits.

It was Friday evening again when the four girls gathered round the display table in the salon and gave themselves sombrely enough to the instructions of Rachel, the oldest girl who had had some experience in spiritualism. Hazel hovered nearby uncertain if they were doing the right thing and anxious that no harm should come from the enterprise. It was through Rachel that some kind of communication was achieved, after they had sat for some time with joined hands and closed eyes.

"They're very cross," Rachel transmitted to the others. "they're very annoyed with us for the last time."

There was a deep silence in the salon while the young hairdressers digested the information. "We were only trying to get through to them, to try and understand why they keep moving things around," whispered the youngest.

"No," said Rachel, her eyes shut close and concentrating hard, "there was something else." She seemed to listen for a long time.

"I know," she said at last, "it was the dummy. That's what they're cross about. We've got to dismantle it."

The effigy still leaned against the wall inside the cupboard where it had been thrown. Hazel brought it into the room and divested the broomstick of its mop and cape. It seemed little enough to get into a frenzy about – three simple objects put together in innocent fun. But Rachel felt as if a load had been taken off her shoulders.

"There won't be any more trouble," she said. "I'm sure of it."

She was right.

The Riddle of the Fields

In the early years of this century, Meg and Thomas Brundle came to take up the tenancy of Moat Farm a few miles from Downham Market in the Fens. They had farmed before but only in the kinder conditions of the south-west and they soon found that such experience was of limited value in this strange, open landscape in which they found themselves. So far as Tom was concerned it was a worthwhile change despite all its drawbacks for the potential of the black soil had been part of his dreams for many a year. In his nature too, there was a certain affinity with the mysterious beauty of that lonely land.

Meg had no such sympathy. To her the landscape seemed not only crude and bare but grossly utilitarian. From the start she had had reservations about the move and when her mother came to the new farm to see the couple settled in, the two women joined in denouncing the situation in which they found themselves. This had not only to do with the climate, the outlook, the prevailing wetness and what they considered to be a general lack of civilised amenities but also with another matter of which they learned only some time after they arrived.

In itself, it was little enough – at least Tom thought so. Something that had happened centuries before and nothing to do with practical, modern farming. After all, there must have been battles all over Britain if you went back far enough and the fact of having a farm on an ancient battle-field was of no great consequence. The matter was only inconvenient in that Meg and her mother insisted that it must be haunted and placed it at the very top of their list of complaints but Tom saw the whole thing as worthy only of sceptical good humour. Anyway, he reasoned, how could anyone tell exactly where the old battlefield was.

He asked the question in the pub one day and was answered by a chorus of guffaws from the static regulars, one of whom was forthcoming enough to take his nose from his glass long enough to pronounce "boons" before immediately replacing it. Knowing smiles illumined one or two faces. Boons, ah, them boons.

"My old father," expanded one of the smilers, "he reckoned they used to fetch human boons by the cartload from the fields on Moat Farm."

"Real human boons," explained another. "You can still plough them up at odd times. Ah, that must have bin a terrible sort o' battle there."

What battle it was that strewed its bones over their fenland fields the locals would have found it hard to determine. It was just "the Battle" and the area it had covered was "the Battlefield", even now after centuries of peace. What they were certain of was that the whole of the Battlefield was haunted and there were tales gruesome and frightening to hear of groaning and shouting in the night, of the sounds of conflict with armour and with horses. No one could rightly swear that he had ever heard anything of the sort himself. It was just something known. It was a queer place.

That night the thoughts of haunted fields kept Tom awake up to an unwonted hour. Even when he eventually drifted off to sleep it seemed but minutes before he was suddenly aroused again by a sound out of doors. Quietly he got out of bed, pulled a coat over his nightshirt and went to the window. He stood there and stared and could not believe what he saw.

In the dark night there was a great patch of soft light spread over the fields. The Battlefield was gleaming as if covered by a silver pool shimmering and changing over acres and acres of ground. Tom was looking out as if petrified when Meg awoke. "What is it?" she wanted to know and came to the window to look. For a few moments she stared disbelievingly then straightway began to dress and to pack a trunk with her belongings, adamant that neither she nor her mother would spend another night in such a house and on such a farm.

When daylight came the fields resumed their normal appearance but it made no difference to Meg's resolve. It was devil's work, she decided. She would never come back until the devil was exorcised and driven off. It was up to Tom to get the parson to use his powers to dispose of the evil. Until that time she would go and live with her mother.

The day that followed was not the happiest in Tom's life. His own shock at seeing the fields covered in that ghostly light was bad enough but to be left alone on the farm and somehow having to 'do something' about it was enough to turn the sober man to drink. When the parson arrived later in the day with bell, book and candle, Tom had already downed a reassuring quantity of rum and he welcomed the man of religion as a drinking frield as well as an exorcisor of ghosts. When darkness eventually settled over the farm and the time for action arrived, the two men were as well fortified with alcohol as their dangerous enterprise demanded.

127

Tom carried a lighted candle in one hand and a hand-bell in the other as steadily as his condition would allow while the parson followed along with a massive Bible.

They were scarcely out of the farmhouse door before they came to a halt. The fields ahead were glowing silver as on the night before, like a great blanket of light in the darkness but it was not this that made them stop. There was something else. A small silver creature shaped like a rabbit came racing out of the lighted field and another dog-like animal covered in glowing silver followed. They were racing one after the other at top speed, then when the larger creature espied the two men it suddenly changed direction and came towards them. Candle and bell and probably also the Book were dropped ignominiously in the farmyard as Tom and the parson ran back into the house, slamming the door on the silver fiend only a yard or two behind. Both men agreed that another bottle of rum would be required to soothe their shaken nerves and to keep away the evils of the night.

It was well into the daylight of the next day when Tom's farming neighbour arrived at Moat Farm, alerted by the postman who claimed he had seen bodies lying in the kitchen. The bodies were there sure enough and it did not take long to diagnose a drunken stupor but a good deal longer to try and bring the two men out of it. A sober regard of the things about them was the last thing that they desired and they returned by slow and unwilling stages to the painful memories of the night before. So obviously out of tune with the everyday world were they that the kindly farmer packed them both off to bed to sleep comfortably until the evening.

By that time, haggard and unkempt though they

128

were, they were in a fair state to contemplate reality. Tom did so and groaned at the trials that had been laid upon him. The parson contemplated, too, and could find little in his conduct that would please a bishop. As for the neighbour, he could scarcely contain his curiosity as to the cause of such behaviour.

Tom decided to tell him all. The tales of ghostly conflict on the Battlefield, the fields that lighted up at night, the terror of creatures coming from the Battlefield enclosed in a hideous luminosity and worst of all, the refusal of his wife to live at the farm until it was all cleared up.

"Good God," said the farmer. He looked from one lined and crestfallen face to the other. "Good God," he said, "I can't believe it."

For a moment Tom thought his neighbour was overcome by the enormity of the problem and was expressing his sympathy. But as the farmer turned away as if to cough the sound of suppressed mirth became unmistakable and in another moment he was throwing his head back and roaring with laughter. It was sometime before he could speak and then it was only to congratulate himself that he had not had such a good laugh for years. Tom began to think him very callous but before he could make any comment the farmer said good-humouredly:

"You have to take a pinch of salt with anything you hear or see about the Fens. It's a strange place and takes some getting used to but there's usually a good explanation. You talk about ghostly noises from the Battlefield at night. Ghostly noises, my foot! I've lived beside the Battlefield all my life and never heard a thing. Now, as for these other ghosts of yours that light the fields up at night – well, get your boots and leggings on and we'll go and see how they're getting on. Bring your dog too, poor old boy, I reckon he'll enjoy a bit of ghost hunting."

Completely mystified and not at all inclined to go too near the silver fields, Tom and the parson followed him out into the darkness. He walked directly to the gate of the first field of light, opened it and walked in. Then he waited until the others came up to the gate.

"You can stop there if you don't want to come in," he said and began to laugh again. "You can stop them trying to escape." He walked up and down a few times in a pool of light that reached from his boots to his knees and then came back to the gate. His boots and leggings were shining silver. So was Tom's dog when he came out from his own investigations and showed himself as the terror of the night before.

"Glow-worms," said the farmer coming up to the two men. "A million of 'em in that field, I should reckon. It's the young clover they like. They settle on the clover, feed on it, breed on it. And in the day-time you don't know they're there. So much for your ghosts. Now, why don't you send for your missus and tell her you can't understand why anyone would be frightened of a few glow-worms in a field?"

James Fairhead's Story

My name is Rosa Fisk. I am the only person that James Fairhead ever told his story to and now that I am getting on in years I think it is right for me to set it down for others to see.

When I was a young woman my mother kept the White Hart at Blythburgh and I was usually busy helping to serve drinks. It was quite a pleasant place to be living in then because there was always some liveliness going on and we liked a bit of excitement to mix with the dull days. A lot of it was connected with the smuggling which I was supposed not to know about but I could always tell when there had been a good run by the amount of liquor that was flowing.

At other times, when things were quiet, the men used to sit together in the parlour and someone would sing a song or more often they would tell stories of their early adventures and of strange happenings. Listening to some of these tales in between bringing in their quarts of ale made me very interested in the old folk-lore traditions of the area. One thing I noticed was that the name of James – or Jim – Fairhead was often mentioned as someone with a story to relate if only he could be persuaded to tell it.

Of course, I knew James Fairhead fairly well, as did everyone else in the village. He was quite old then, getting on for seventy I should think. When he came into the White Hart he hardly ever stayed for long and never joined in the story-telling. So far as I know, he was a bachelor all his life.

Well, I was young and full of curiosity in them days and well-favoured enough to know I could turn a few heads if I'd a mind to. Many a time I made a bit of extra fuss of Jimmy when he came in, hoping I would get a chance to ask him for his story. But somehow, what with one excuse or another, he always got out of it.

Then one day during the harvest time I got the chance I had been waiting for. It was good weather and all the men were out mowing the corn. My mother called me and said: "Will you take Jimmy Fairhead his fourses? He's mowing the barley all on his own in the stackyard field." She then handed me a pewter jug of porter and some fourses cakes and off I went.

The stackyard field was quite a small field and Jimmy was bent over his scythe working on his own but when he saw me he soon gathered up a bundle of barley and sat down. I gave him the vittles and sat down beside him. After a few minutes talk about other things I asked him to tell me his story. He was a bit upset at first. Although it was something that happened long before, he still found it difficult to talk about it.

"Even now," he said, "after all these years, something goes down my back and makes me shiver when I only just think about it."

Then after a little silence he agreed to tell me what he had never told anyone else except his mother and she was now long dead. This is Jimmy Fairhead's story:

When I was only eighteen or nineteen, some of us young lads from round here used to go to Lowestoft for the fishing. We worked on the trawlers and such like, sometimes for short trips but there was one long

132

voyage each year that would last from October nearly to Christmas. One problem was how to get to Lowestoft and how to get back. Sometimes we got a lift on the carrier's cart but other times it might happen he'd only got room for our kit and we had to walk. One thing about the long voyage was that we could usually catch the mail cart out of Lowestoft and that would bring us home to Blythburgh soon after daylight in the morning.

The time I'm thinking of, there was a chap by the name of George Burton lived in the village. You may have heard of him – he was a master chap for devilry. He was in everything that was dangerous provided it brought him a bit of profit and he was deep in the smuggling business. Many a cask of spirits arrived by way of George Burton and he used to work hand in glove with that Mrs. Gildersleeves of Leiston. They used to say that she would cover up kegs of brandy under her crinoline.

Well, one morning I came back from the long voyage and got as far as the White Hart just as that was getting clear daylight. I then had to walk up to my mother's cottage and in doing so I had to go past George Burton's place. That was one of them odd-looking houses you sometimes see end-on to the road and standing right close to the roadside. That was only a tiny little place, wattle-and-daub and thatch. Gone now, I'm glad to say. George lived there in that little old cottage with his mother.

I was walking along cheerful enough and glad to get home. I'd got my kit-bag on my shoulder and a string of herrings for my mother in my right hand and just as I got near to George's house I saw him standing there. He was leaning up against the wall beside the road, just under the thatched eaves and he was standing right still.

When I got up to him on the other side of the road, I said: "Hullo, George. You're about in good time this morning! What deviltry have you been up to to get you out so early?"

He never answered. That surprised me a bit. I said: "Aren't you going to speak to me?" He still didn't say anything. I came to a halt on the other side of the road to where he was standing. That sort of riled me to think he wouldn't take any notice of me. I asked him again if he was going to answer but he took no notice. So I said: "If you don't speak I'll come over there and souse you across the skull with these herrings."

He still didn't speak. I crossed the road towards him and I swung the string of herrings with my right hand to give him a good clout across the skull. The herrings went right through him, hit on the wall and he just vanished as I stood there.

Well, that properly knocked me out then. I can't tell you how I felt but I was so weak I could hardly walk and how I got to my poor old mother's house I don't know. We lived in one of the red brick cottages near the school then. I managed to reach the house and I was in such a state I just sort of fell in the door.

As it happened, Mother was just coming down the stairs. I must have been a proper sight because she gave me a good look, then she said: "You drunken young varmint. That's a nice way to come home after all these weeks away."

"Mother," I said, "I aren't drunk."

"Well that certainly look like it," she said.

"I've seen a apparation," I said. She still did not seem to believe me.

"Apparition?" she said, "apparition indeed. And where did you see this apparition?"

Then I begun to tell her about George Burton not speaking to me and how I swung the herrings at him but I could tell by the way she was looking at me there was something else about it that I didn't know.

"Don't be such a fule," she said, "talking like that about George Burton. Why he was took bad and died and was buried in the church yard nearly a month ago."

After mother had made us some tea and we had talked about it she still seemed half disbelieving.

I said: "Well, you go along to George Burton's house and you'll see on the wall there where I hit out."

"Come on then, boy, and show me where," she said.

"Not me, Mother, I wouldn't go back along that road to save my life. You'll have to go alone, Mother."

Well, she did. She walked back to the Burton cottage and looked at the wall and she could see the fish scales where I'd hit out at George. She believed me then.

We only lived half a mile from the Burtons but I never went along that road again, not even to this very day and I'm an old man now. There have been times when I've had to walk miles out of my way to avoid that place and I shall do so till I can't walk any more."

That was James Fairhead's story. Then he scrambled to his feet and said: "Lawk-a-mussy, here have I been yarning with you all this while and the master said I was to mow this field afore I went home."

An Unforgettable Night

It was the early spring of 1950. My mother had just died after many years of nursing, leaving me very much alone. At that time my home was in London and to get right away for a holiday I decided to go back to my native area. Exactly where that is I do not intend to say as it could possibly embarrass my friends there. Sufficient to say that an old school pal named Nancy had invited me to come and stay with her family for as long as I wished and to make their home my base for visiting some of the other people that I remembered.

The weather was exceptionally warm and fine for April. It seemed a good idea to take a bus and spend a whole day in familiar haunts looking up one or two old acquaintances. First among them, of course, would be Mary because we had spent quite a lot of our early life together and for some years I had lived almost next door to her. Later we lost contact for some time but I knew that she had married and had a daughter who, by my calculations must be somewhere near twenty by now.

It is surprising how remembered scenes seem to change in the mind. I could have sworn I knew the area where Mary lived like the back of my hand, yet when I got there I felt that it had got changed about somehow. It took me a lot longer than I expected to find the old address and when I reached it at last the

137

door opened at my knock and a strange face came into view. Yes, Mary had moved but not too far away. The present tenant gave me exact directions and I proceeded to walk there, getting more and more conscious of time slipping away and of the likelihood of seeing all my friends that day becoming more remote. Mary's home now turned out to be the top flat in a modest-sized house and to my great relief she was at home and delighted to see me.

There was so much of our younger days to remember and chat over, so many mutual friends of the past to be recalled and brought up to date that there was no hope of going much further that day. Mary suggested that I should telephone the friends with whom I was staying and tell them that I would not return until the next day. It was something I readily agreed to. I had no sort of premonition at that moment that all was not well and that this night would turn out to be the worst of my life.

During the evening I left Mary's flat to visit one or two of the neighbours that I knew and got back again at about a quarter past eleven. Mary came down to open the door and on going upstairs I noticed that the lights were on in every room as well as the hall and when she ushered me into the lounge she did not turn any of the other lights off.

Perhaps it is only a kind of superstition on my part but I have always associated my misfortunes with the colour green. I had been a bit taken aback to see that Mary's carpet and suite were all in green. There was a rather unsettled atmosphere in the room but I told myself I was just feeling on edge because I did not like the colour.

When we eventually stopped talking it must have

been around 1 a.m. and we went through to the kitchen where Mary filled a large stone hot water bottle for me, using kettles full of boiling water. She explained that her husband was usually away at night because of his job as a long-distance lorry-driver and since her daughter too was living away from home there was plenty of sleeping space. She told me the room that I could use and carried the hot water bottle, wrapped in a towel because it was so hot, along to my bed.

The room contained a single bed with the window on its immediate left. The window was fitted with a black roller blind which was already pulled down. At the other end of the room was a wardrobe, in line with the door leading out into the hall. I asked Mary for a tumbler of water and placed it on a chair beside the bed and beneath the window. Thinking to be kind, Mary offered me a green cardigan as the room was cold but I declined it with thanks. As there was no bedside lamp, she suggested that I should undress and get into bed and she would put the light off at the switch just inside the door. She left the door ajar and I saw the hall light go out just after she said goodnight.

A little later it seemed to me that the room was rather chilly and I reached down to put my feet on the hot water bottle. It was cold, yet only a short time before it had been so hot it could not be touched with bare hands. As I was wondering about this, the blind suddenly became illuminated with a pale grey light. Looking for a reasonable explanation and determined not to be upset by such details I decided that there must be a house opposite and someone had just switched on a light. (I discovered next morning that there was no house opposite but by that time so many strange things had happened that it did not surprise me in the least.)

In the meantime the room was becoming even colder and with an eerie atmosphere that I could not shake off. I put my left hand out and grasped the tumbler to have a drink as my mouth had become very dry. At the same moment I realised that there was something else in the room. A shapeless dark object, seen only by the thin grey light from the blind, had come through the half open door and now seemed to be coming towards me. I was petrified with fear.

The glass of water was still in my shaking hand. Suddenly it was knocked with terrific force from underneath so that it shot up and hit the ceiling, showering me with water and broken glass. I tried to call out but found I could not utter a sound. In a panic I dived under the bedclothes but then realised that it was a stupid thing to do as I could get smothered. A quick look around showed the creature standing in the doorway, then moving as if going into the hall. Was it going away, I wondered, or was it just waiting there? Somehow or other I must get to the light switch by the door while I had a chance.

Just at that moment the light on the blind went out, plunging the room into complete darkness. It seemed more urgent than ever to reach the switch but I knew that the bedside rug must be covered with broken glass and water so I could not get out of the bed that way. The only alternative was to crawl to the bottom of the bed and climb over the end of it. I could feel glass on the bedcover and had the presence of mind to shake it over the floor at the side. Quaking with terror, I crawled to the foot of the bed and over on to the floor. I could not tell where the monster was or whether he

140

would spring upon me from the darkness at any moment but I knew that I had to get the light on. At last I could feel the wall and then the switch and knew the utter relief of being able to see – but it was only for a few moments. As I turned my back to the door to survey the mess of broken glass on the rug there was a click behind me and the light went off again.

Now I was standing in the middle of the room in my bare feet and with pitch-black darkness all around. I could not go forward because of the glass nor backward because of the horror that seemed to be waiting behind me. For many seconds during which I seemed to be frozen with fear, I just stood there. Then I decided that I must feel my way slowly to the foot of the bed and climb over in the same way that I had got out.

After much fumbling in the dark and shuffling very carefully with my feet, I reached the bed. It seemed to reassure me, though it was not necessarily a place of safety. I climbed on to the bed and lay there shaking, not knowing if something unbelievably horrible was going to happen. The hours drifted slowly by until the first light began to show at the sides of the blind. It was the most welcome dawn I have ever known. As the daylight grew the eerie atmosphere died away, the room became warmer and in the feeling of relief I suddenly felt as if I had aged a good many years during the night.

It was about 7.30 when Mary came into the room and stood at the foot of the bed. The first thing she asked was: "What sort of night did you have – did anything odd happen?" Well, plenty of odd things had happened but it struck me as very strange that she should ask this question. I countered with: "What sort of things?"

She came and sat on the bed and I realised that I was going to hear a good deal more about this haunted room than she had told me yesterday. She began by asking if I had noticed that all the lights in her flat were blazing when I arrived. It was because she was frightened, she said. She had once spent a night in this same room and seen some bulky shape moving and on many other occasions she had seen the shadowy-black thing hovering between the bathroom, which was next door, and the bedroom.

She admitted that she had deliberately put me in that haunted room without any warning and she wanted to know exactly what had happened. When I told her, she actually smiled as if it were good news and at first I felt very resentful at having been put through such an ordeal which was by no means amusing to me.

"I couldn't tell you," Mary said, "because I had to get proof that I was not the only one to experience this." She told me that for months past it had been a source of unpleasant scenes with her husband who not only scorned the idea of a ghost or some such manifestation but accused her of having hallucinations and of being mentally unbalanced. Now that it was proved otherwise, she could not help beaming with delight and relief. As for me, the experiences of that dreadful night went very deep and in the next few weeks I watched my hair become completely white.

The Last Candle at Clare

It was no ordinary ghost but the master of evil himself who came to Clare on that day when the Sacrist of the Priory betrayed his trust. The Sacrist heard the cloven hoofs clear on the floor of the empty church when the fatal bargain was made but could not extricate himself because of his greed.

At that time the old disciplines and ideals of the religious houses were crumbling everywhere and being supplanted by indolence and selfishness. The process was hastened at Clare by the appointment of a new Prior with a decidedly permissive attitude. Galfridus followed the coarser ways of the world and hunted and feasted with little inclination for the dry duties of administration or for over-seeing the friars in their separate duties. In a short time the atmosphere of irresponsibility was communicated to the whole of that once rigorously-run establishment. Not least among those to desert the high standards of the past was the Sacrist, Hugh of Bury. In his keeping reposed the church treasures and ornate vestments given by wealthy Suffolk landowners and wool merchants as proof of their piety.

Much of this treasure was locked away since it was not required for regular use and for this purpose a great old iron chest with a complex set of locks was held under the care of the Sacrist. Among the valuables in the chest was a cope adorned with jewels, which had once been donated to the Priory. There were also offerings in cash contributed over a considerable period. It was the Sacrist's duty to keep detailed accounts of all monies and how they were used and of other materials such as the devotional candles, which he issued as required.

Hugh was soon seduced by the Prior's example into giving way to selfish thought of his own needs and into contemplation of the unused wealth within the chest. He found that he was able to make some kind of compromise with his own conscience by deciding to use the valuables to raise a loan, promising himself that before the date of redemption he would somehow manage to buy the goods back. So, the jewelled cope and many other fine pieces of church property, found their way into the hands of the usurers.

Poor Hugh of Barry was no practised wrong-doer. In earlier times his punctilious devotions and ungrudged self-denial followed the best traditions of the friars. Now, the price of his back-sliding was the heavy weight that accompanied his thoughts throughout the day and night. There were periods of black despair in which he had to admit to himself that the chest was losing more and more of its contents and that he was unlikely ever to get them back. Worse still was the fear that the depredations would soon be discovered – not by the indolent Prior, perhaps, but by some official visitor. The Pope's Legate had visited Bury St. Edmunds recently. If he also came to Clare the likelihood was that he would examine the Priory possessions in detail. To Hugh's spiritual credit it must be said that all of these worldly considerations, bad enough as they were, came only second to his deep, inescapable self-despite at having betrayed his trust.

Such gloomy thoughts depressed the Sacrist constantly, even on the fishing days. With their house so pleasantly near the river Stour it was a regular routine of the friars to combine the religious requirement of contemplation with the lazy enjoyment of fishing but even in such circumstances there was little contentment for Hugh. Sitting by the river bank one afternoon as the dusk began to create thin clouds of mist above the water, he realised suddenly that his fishing companions had already gone and left him there deep in thought. He was preparing to follow when he saw the figure of a monk before him. The monk was wearing a habit unfamiliar to Hugh, with skirts that covered his feet and a cowl kept so close it was impossible to see his face. However, he had a very friendly manner and addressed a few cheery words of greeting to the Sacrist, who felt that here was a very sympathetic fellow indeed.

He had been a Sacrist himself, the monk said. He knew how onerous the task was and how difficult to keep proper accounts. Perhaps from his own experience he could help Hugh to lighten the burden which seemed to be weighing on his mind. The Sacrist pondered for a moment attempting unsuccessfully to see the monk's face under the dark cowl. Then, finding it a relief to be able to confess to one so understanding of human faults, he told of his transgressions in the matter of the church property and of his fear that eventually the loss would be known and his good name gone for ever.

"Well," said the monk, "It is a sad thing to see anyone so cast down as you seem to be and I want to help you if I can. I happen to know a way out of your difficulty. It is quite simple and would provide you with enough money to buy back the vestments and have some over for yourself."

"I wonder if such a miracle could ever happen?"

"Yes, indeed. And no great miracle after all. As the Sacrist you havecharge of the candles? Then follow this simple advice. When you sell someone a candle and it is lit, extinguish it again as soon as the person leaves. Sell it again to the next who comes and to the next and the next and all will pay you in full for the same candle. Then, sell all the new candles from your store, and claim that the mice have eaten them and you need more. Soon you will have so many candles you will need others to sell them for you."

The idea filled Hugh with renewed hope and the few misgivings that he felt he soon managed to dispel. He uttered his heartfelt thanks to his new friend and asked if there was something he could do for him in return.

"There is nothing I need," replied the monk, "my reward lies in removing that unhappiness that I saw on your countenance. But just to remind you of me and of this meeting I would like you to keep one of the candles and remember that that candle is mine. Let it be the first half-burned candle that you take from the Shrine. It shall be a talisman and as long as you keep it for me all will go well for you. But if you should ever light that candle and let it burn down to the very last flicker of light – at that last moment you would have to pay the price."

"Do not worry," said Hugh, "I will keep the first candle and remember that it is yours. It is a small thing to do."

The idea that the monk had propounded was so simple and so easily accomplished that Hugh set to work immediately. He sold his candles to the many who came to the church, the sick and the faithful, the priest and the sinner and none of those who lit a candle stayed for longer than the length of a prayer. It was an easy matter to put out the candles and sell them again to the next comer and the next. And twice in one week he claimed that all his candles had been eaten by mice and ordered a great many more. Soon he had so many candles he sent them to be sold in the town and quickly acquired enough money to redeem the jewelled cope.

One thing he remembered above all else. The very first candle that he took half-burned from the Shrine he carried carefully to his own cell and set it on the window ledge there. It was a trivial thing but as he had promised, so it would be. He could have spared the monk a hundred candles if he had wanted them. Yet, as time went by, and month after month saw an increase in the Sacrist's private wealth, the small, solitary candle became covered in dust and he could scarcely remember what he had kept it for.

By this time the general resources of the Priory, thanks to a debilitating laziness and widespread pilfering throughout, were becoming so run-down that even Galfridus began to be alarmed. A superficial inspection of the various departments of the Friary showed serious losses in stock. In particular the cellarer, the larderer and the Sacrist were severely reprimanded – the latter for using too many candles. For his punishment Hugh was to be confined to the Friary for a month, with half of that period to be sustained only by bread and water. In addition, he was required to hand the key of the candle store over to the sub-Sacrist.

147

Hugh considered that his punishment was over-severe, particularly as the Prior was off again on one of his thoughtless hunting forays with many of the friars in attendance. Alone, he carried out the few duties that were left to him and waited with some resentment for the hunters to return. That day the Prior, with all the retinues of fellow sportsmen, of horses and hounds and sundry followers, was expected to return at about dusk, when every man and especially the Prior himself would be hungry and demand to be served with food and drink at once. It was not the Sacrist's place to deal with this, except that the precious supply of salt was in his care and when he heard the huntsmen returning he suddenly remembered that he had been asked to get some more salt from the cellar.

The daylight was slowly dying outside and in the Friary it was already difficult to see. In the cellar it would be pitch black. Without his key, Hugh could not get a candle from the store but in his hurry recalled a candle standing on the window shelf of his room. Fearful of any further reprimands of laziness, he quickly lit the candle and went to the cellar. He fancied he could already hear the Prior calling for food and drink and in his haste he snatched some salt but left the candle in the cellar still alight.

It was only a small candle and did not take long to burn down to the last drop of wax, the last flicker of light. Hugh happened to be on the refectory steps at that moment and before him was the figure of the strange monk. What happened then no one could tell but there were frightful screams that brought the friars running from the refectory, only to find the Sacrist dead at the foot of the steps. There was a smell of sulphur in the air and the sound of cloven hoofs. There could be no profit in saying a mass over that lost soul.